WORDS
LIKE
THUNDER

Made in Michigan Writers Series

GENERAL EDITORS

Michael Delp, Interlochen Center for the Arts
M. L. Liebler, Wayne State University

A complete listing of the books in this series can be found online at
wsupress.wayne.edu

WORDS LIKE THUNDER

NEW AND USED ANISHINAABE PRAYERS

LOIS BEARDSLEE

Wayne State University Press
Detroit

ISBN 978-0-8143-4748-5 (paperback)
ISBN 978-0-8143-4749-2 (e-book)

Library of Congress Control Number: 2020931209

Publication of this book was made possible by a generous
gift from The Meijer Foundation. This work is supported
in part by an award from the Michigan Council for Arts
and Cultural Affairs.

Wayne State University Press

Leonard N. Simons Building
4809 Woodward Avenue
Detroit, Michigan 48201-1309

Visit us online at wsupress.wayne.edu

CONTENTS

GEOGRAPHIC ANALYSIS OF HEARTS AND LUNGS OF HOLOCAUST SURVIVORS

DARK DAYS, LONG NIGHTS

WORDS LIKE THUNDER

BESKIKWE

FOLDED-OVER WOMAN

When she was little, her mother would pick raspberries into a very small bowl. Her mother explained that this saved her back from getting sore and prevented heat exhaustion. As a child, she knew nothing of heat stroke and the necessity of maximizing hours in an overly demanding day. So, she slipped in and out of the berry patch and lakes and streams and shook water onto her mother's loose housedress. Her mother trotted back and forth between the berry patch and the house, where she spread out the berries to clean them. In this way, Folded-Over Woman learned about harvesting the world around her. Her world smelled of mushroom omelets and great, heaping, tart fruit pies. Her world was abundance.

Folded-Over Woman trots back into her own kitchen with a small glass bowl, heaped, pressed against her nightshirt, with a hand cupped at the outside to keep its contents from tumbling out into the tall grass. She spreads out the bowl's contents thinly into a pie pan to allow insects to crawl to the top—tiny strong-smelling leaflike bugs and miniscule larvae from small pale-green moths. She sorts out overripe, intoxicating fruits bearing larvae, and these she deposits next to the hidden bowlful of rainwater she has set apart against the side of the house for frogs and toads. She does this with each bowlful of berries, each batch resting in turn while she gulps cold water, then picks the next.

The raspberries are tumbling into Folded-Over Woman's hands, and she cups a palm under the lowest of full clusters first, as she had been taught by her mother and her own childhood experience. Only take the berries that come loose easily, her mother had taught her, so that the ripest don't fall into obscurity and grit. Folded-Over Woman misses her mother's voice. She misses having someone else to take responsibility for her in the heat, while she tries to maximize her time and her resources. She has been picking since the light was low, and the berries all looked dark and ripe. To reach hidden fruits below her knees, she folds herself over even more, and she daydreams about walking upright.

Raspberries are tumbling into Folded-Over Woman's hands, ripening and available faster than she can keep up with them. She doesn't know how to divide her cool mornings between obligations. She needs to pick sweetgrass so that she can hide in her house and make baskets rather than try to be a housekeeper for strangers, rather than try to survive outside of this microcosm.

Folded-Over Woman gently lifts and tilts back delicate, brittle green canes to garner their gifts, praying not to snap off fruit cluster heads, wanting to leave treasures available after her own harvest. She rests on her heels, patient, sharing a spreading, lower world of foliage with delicate wasps that suck juice from dark fruits—like her, hovering, and hungry for opportunity, for continuity, and for forever.

Folded-Over Woman presses sweat away from her eyes, as she fingers wilted cane tops, broken fruiting clusters, drying, wasting effort on the part of the plants. And now she sees there are no flowers left on the clusters in the overwhelming heat. She doesn't remember seeing the raspberries flower. Perhaps she had been too busy being greedy with wild strawberries. Perhaps she had been harvesting an early batch of sweetgrass, competing with heat and distance and obligations; but she'd missed it. She'd missed reveling in that bloom. That had never happened before. She had never given away that piece of herself before. She had always watched for the blooms—first the black-caps, close to the house, bringing joy to her children while they listened to woodcocks' spiraling beeps and musical descent; then red-raspberries on the partially shaded slope, where they'd listened for catbirds and pollinating bees. Folded-Over Woman doesn't remember clumsily breaking off immature fruits or delicate canes. Now they are there for no one. Perhaps she had simply crushed them by sitting down, out of exhaustion, unable to keep bending herself over and over, her spine compressing from responsibility—responsibility for children and future generations, for other species, for other people, for other people's behaviors and attitudes, for racism and hate. She feels too tired and disempowered to take responsibility for small daily dramas in her own small berry patch.

And Folded-Over Woman wipes tears of salty sweat from her eyes. She cries, surprised, resisting at first. Quiet. Wiping away sweat and hurt, fear and helplessness, immobilizing confusion and lack of opportunity. Folded-Over Woman rains onto wilted raspberry canes in the heat of oppression. And for the first time in seven years, since her youngest child had been wrenched from her arms, Folded-Over Woman cries out loud and thunders back at clouded-over skies, black hearts, and empty souls that surround her berry survival patch. She rises and unfolds. Formerly generous berry thorns tear at the thin, old fabric of her nightshirt, and faded red plaid shreds under the pull of Folded-Over Woman's constricted, sore muscles. Salted waters stream into soaked, shredded fabric of exhaustion and desperation while she rises up, tall, above well-established thorny canes and restrictive social norms. Folded-Over Woman stretches upward with berry-stained, grasping fingers into sister spruce boughs, heavy with wind against darkening skies. She is joined in her indignation by grasslands and forests full of insects and shrieking toad women swollen with rage and necessity. Electricity streaks from open hearts and mouths into heavy, oppressive airs. Cloud breath bursts down toward her angry, expectant berry patch.

A wet Indian woman is like a lightning rod.

ODEMINIGIIZIS

A POEM ABOUT PICKING WILD STRAWBERRIES
WITH AN ENGLISH TRANSLATION

Folded-Over Woman's wild strawberry days are long and ripe as she
celebrates cool mornings, harvesting and tasting and commandeering
scents like entitlements.

It is a good year for strawberries.

Rag of an old nightshirt grasps thighs and shoulders and long, soft
breasts, mature tree branches deepening with time, waiting out her
solstice.

She's already made a strawberry pie.

She unfolds that bold head upward into gracious gifts of air-moving
clouds and thunder pushing against her horizon, eyes bold and
sideways and dark, ready to push back.

She is deep and mounded.

Folded-Over Woman's dogs have barked down thunder for
generations, tearing at groins overhead, sidling up to her desperation
in empty spaces where calm lives like shallow breath.

Dogs always bark at thunder.

Even lightning bolts lick wild strawberries out of Folded-Over
Woman's outstretched palms, pushing back generations of wind to
steal salt from her skin.

Skin is all she has left.

Folded-Over Woman wills her head into the clouds, leafed-out treetop in a demanding breeze, shaking her long hair—first to the sun, then down to strawberry earth.

Her clouds are blackening and thick like jam.

She puts clouds in her mouth if they smash when she pulls or they've dried like strong words, ignored by men and animals by virtue of her weak status and tenuous brown roots.

She is followed by thunder.

When her children were small, alive, running like insects, she willed them to put two into their mouths, one into a basket, any basket. Together they consumed the sky, like gods.

The rain is scattered, sometimes gentle.

Folded-Over Woman stands, hunches, crouches, reaches, sweeps the inches crowding the earth as though they are her own, pinching fruits from the mouths of insects and birds.

She will pick as long as she dares.

Her fingers are like thieves, grasping life and comfort and joy in small, fragrant bursts, curling in on herself in her own cool, kind wind, swaddled in solstice heat.

She harvests as though she has a future.

Dog-woman, she's doubled over, smelling for red, smelling for ripeness, smelling for comfort, affluence and joy, purpose and peace; smelling for tomorrow, where photosynthesis only dries in summer's heat.

She keeps looking for resources.

Rag of an old nightshirt pinching up raindrops, big and berry-full, cool, harsh, and demanding; thunder talks back and spits in her eyes.

Better stay down low.

Folded-Over Woman tosses upward her easy and soft words, strawberry-breath warm gifts to wet breezes, prayers to dark skies, smiles to power and electrical forces.

Rain is respite from any heat.

Folded-Over Woman hovers, shelters the basket, shelters her fruit, shelters her own womb, crouching against the excess of a summer storm, hoping to find safety in the assured recurrence of the pain of imminent heat.

Chilled, she waits for the devil she knows.

Her hopes are like crows staring upward for sharp-beaked hawks to open springtime's carcass, so that she can snatch sweet flesh and stuff tomorrows into her threadbare pockets.

She is an outsider in a world of plenty.

Folded-Over Woman releases her own fruits to the winds and gurgles in celebration of her own ability to find sustenance in mouthfuls of cloudfuls of wind-borne grit.

She has experienced forced sterilization through socioeconomic inequality.

Her long toes scratch out habitat for seedlings and trail wispy runners to horizons, pounding seeds into expectant soil.

She never gives up.

Folded-Over Woman looks sideways, spreading satisfaction and safety like waves of rain and heat while harsh sentiments curl upward, seeking her long, bare ankles.

A wet Indian woman is like a lightning rod.

THE ANISHINAABE CHILDREN'S STRAWBERRY-PICKING RULE

When I was small, my mother had only one strawberry-picking rule:
For every berry you put into the bowl, you put two into your mouth.
I used to think it was the best rule in the whole world
Until I started to burp, and I fled to the far side of the patch
Where I could invisibly put more of those berries into that bowl.
I learned to lick my red fingers when a berry slid into mush between them,
Finding enough satisfaction in that constant reminder of the power of small fruit.
Each time I'd stand to stretch, I'd bring the contents up below my nose,
Inhaling hard,
The essence carrying me through our mornings together.
Close.
Together and loving.

When I was in my twenties, and I finally knew everything,
I set my mother straight on that old rule about berries.
It had been fun; but berries were best for the baskets of old-fashioned women
And mounded pies or jam.
She said it was the Anishinaabe mother's berry-picking rule
As she rose up to stretch and slid red jars of memory into my youthful ignorance.
I set her straight on everything:
On social skills, on proper dress, on the world's expectations,
On how to pass for anything but an Anishinaabe mother.
Distant.
Ashamed and disappointed.

She said it was the Anishinaabe mother's berry-picking rule,
And she said it might take patient generations for me to get it right.

Odeminigiizis II

Folded-Over Woman picks wild strawberries in the cool of low light, shaded mornings and evenings,

Grasping at the wingtips of solstice, spread out relentlessly before her in painful, moisture-sucking heat.

Each time Folded-over Woman passes through the shadow of crow mother's nest, mother crow calls out to her,

Loud and raspy, screaming in terror for the welfare of her children, relentless and desperate.

Father crow swoops down low, making a single wasteful pass before he prays out loud for survival of his offspring.

And so, crows growl deep and low, loud and bear-like, left with no arsenal other than bluff and prayer.

Mother and father rasp argumentatively back and forth in desperation, and mother crow caws out until her crow-throat is dry and sterile.

Folded-Over Woman wishes she knew how to put out water or carrion where mother crow might feel safe enough to dip for it,

To continue crying out for safety, as a job, a mission, the only way she knows how to contribute to crow children's well-being.

It is what she has to do, Folded-Over Woman understands.

Folded-Over Woman used to cry raspy and loud, crow-like, too,

To protect her children. But they were plucked away from life and home

By forces more mal-intended than mere berry-picking loners grasping berry soils or sacred, bending treetops.

Offspring lost to pickers of souls, pickers of children, soft and ripe, meaty and ready,

Folded-Over Woman picks wild strawberries in the shadow of croaks and desperate calls.

It is her job, her mission, her only option. It is what she has to do.

She only knows how to glean.

There is no room between thick gusts of throaty desperation for fortune or anchoring grasses and leaves.

Folded-Over Woman can only leave enough wild strawberries for waxwings, for desperate crow people.

Folded-Over Woman understands again and again. She doubles over again and again.

She shares with her whole body.

For a few cool morning moments, she unfolds and sings crow rasps that echo bluing skies and want for survival.

No one gives mother crows the respect they deserve.

MISKIWIIMINIGIIZIS

(ENGLISH TRANSLATION: RASPBERRY-PICKING MOON)
(OJIBWE TRANSLATION: HURT-PICKING MOON)

Raspberries are oppressive cloud cover rolling into her wishful bowl
hands,
Folded-Over Woman raining sweat
Onto eager biology, desperate for blood-rain sustenance.

She should have picked them yesterday.
But she was cleaning and curing sweetgrass from the morning before,
When she'd plucked survival from a small, safe corner in moist soil.

She should have picked them the day before that.
But she was dancing naked in a hollow,
Raining blood into sacred sweetgrass in exchange for its soul.

Heavy skies shove black-capped fruit to her fingertips,
And she might have unfolded herself to close in on them
Only days ago.

Blackcaps race down finger paths of sweetness and heartbreak
Pushing forth rain and dewdrops and feeding-moths
Hungry for survival.

Black- and red-blooded lives stretch themselves outward
From clouded-over wombs of oppressive humidity and heat,
Smiling babies with rolls of fat and eyes rolling toward thunder.

Raspberry growth dances baby-making toward grateful sunshine
As Folded-Over Woman rains her salts over withered offspring,
Strained and starved outside of raspberry-leaf wombs.

She should have pushed back two days before yesterday.
But she was trying to make herself cry into empty strawberry leaf-wombs
While all around her tired grasses yellowed and still sang skyward.

Raspberries are oppressive cloud cover rolling into her wishful bowl hands,
Folded-Over Woman raining sweat
Onto eager biology, desperate for blood-rain sustenance.

She should have given birth to them a day before.
But she was harvesting heat and humidity,
Sheltering generations under threat of extinction.

Broken survival exhales saturated winds over evaporative biology,
Folded-Over Woman raining amniotic fluid
Onto stubborn shaded growth, desperate for blood-rain illumination.

She might have tried to harvest them a week before sunshine.
But she was hiding under the flagellating arms of a spruce tree
Waiting for cloud cover to break open for her fecundity.

WILD RASPBERRIES IN THE RAIN

Folded-Over Woman has been picking wild raspberries since daylight was bold enough to grace her with opportunity.

Gray clouds folded themselves over upon her making her dare to leave windows and doors wide-open to opportunity.

She cowered, in a rain-soaked nightshirt, plaid, flannel, red, over-sized, and gifted for free from the macaroni world of a food bank.

When the children were little and alive, she spent those hours with them, picking essence into their teacups, after game- and word-dips into stored away comfort.

Today, she hard-coffee'd her way out, away from the road, away from incursions into her plans for love and full hearts.

The cup became an opportunity, after her palm was full, and that cup had become as empty as over-used hearts.

Folded-Over Woman picked wild raspberries in molecules of moisture trapped between the hard squeeze of heavy air and the shifting of winds.

Over and over the coffee-less cup filled itself with ripeness and sweetness and hunger and desperation.

As she spread out thinly each cupful of hurt and denigration and, yes, even hope, onto an old pie tin,

For desperate stick bugs and lesser beings to rise to the surface during each successive picking.

Folded-Over Woman has been picking wild raspberries since daylight was bold enough to grace her with opportunity.

She wrings heavy, windless drizzle from the gifted red plaid that dresses her underemployment after-dark and before-opportunity

While she waits for the competition of summer's heat to limit her access to the opportunities of memories of children and hopefulness,

And she sings prayers to wild berries and hours spent with others in a time when small handfuls of great joys filled her hours and ambitions.

Through trees, she is briefly interrupted by voices on the nearby road and her memories of comfort dissolve into Spandex.

Folded-Over Woman folds back in upon herself until she can remember being alone with the cup and the raspberries.

Folded-Over Woman is grateful for each small rise of trees with its gift of shelter from otherness and challenge,

And she closes her ears, dimmed eyes reaching for deep red life, red fruits, red hope, and moist, red opportunity under darkening skies.

Folded-Over Woman welcomes her soft black rain, like opportunity for respite from drought and otherness and opportunities squandered on tomorrow's fruits.

INDIAN CORN

They are not the small, rice-like pointed kernels of Anishinaabe corn
She glimpsed shaken to the surface of precious old coffee cans
In the kitchens of older Indian ladies
Without land to plant and renew them.
Afraid to share them with anybody,
Lest outside people steal their genetic potential and cultural relevance.

She replaces lost future generations with homegrown flint corn from
store-bought seed
Modified in genetic availability for its ornamental and entertainment
potentials
As a symbol of America's love affair with all things old-Indian
Traditional or not.
But they are pretty good,
And she grinds blue and red seed beads in an Osterizer of self-
determination.

She sifts and sorts proteins and starches into fulfilling days and nights
Today, during a rainstorm of low light, self-absorption, and
immobilizing fear.
She fills tall mason jars from the kitchens of older Indian ladies
With dry satisfaction,
Planning for cornbread's flour and winter's grits
And a fine powder to mix with warm milk and cinnamon during
thunderous times.

Odatagaagomiinike

Blackberry Picking

Long, purpled groping digits, blackening by the handfuls
She unfolds herself just enough to grasp back at strong, harsh canes
Reaching from earth to sky in thorny arcs
Piercing Folded-Over Woman's sky-lungs
Lungs moist with late-summer monsoons
Lungs heavy with voice.

Darkening clouds of long, blackening, digit-berries unrolling by the
handfuls
She releases, un-tenses; grasps for sustenance and soothing
Spanning from earth to sky in easy, wind-swept arcs
Saturating senses in every direction
Oxygen-rich, intoxicating thunder-threatening breathfuls
Skies heavy with voice.

Thickening skies, blackening as late-summer fruits
She unfolds darkness just enough to grasp at hopeful downpours
Evaporated up from earth to sky in endless hoops and cycles of
security
Elevating Folded-Over Woman's ambitions
From drought to cool nights, heavy dews, and rainstorms
Steady rains heavy with voice.

Long, white-cloud afternoons, blackening by the handfuls
She unfolds herself just enough to grasp for wild-dog paths
Trotting lightly from earth to sky in easy, sustenance-swept meanders
Guiding Folded-Over Woman from overgrazed barrenness
To survival, regrowth, and shady forever
Resurgence heavy with voice.

Tired, blackened, overused by the handfuls

She unfolds herself just enough to grasp at residual shaded raspberries
Flown up from earth to sky in drumbeat wingfuls
Filling Grouse Woman's poplar-thicket dreams
Dreams full of tomorrow's generations
Dreams heavy with voice.

Thorn-seared flesh, healing by the palmful
She unfolds herself just enough to grasp at solstice's limitations
Stretching up from earth to sky in cautious thunder-whispers
No longer too much even for Grouse Woman's battered-wing dream-
family
Limitations filling Folded-Over Woman's sensibilities with sharing
Sharing heavy with voice.

Torn-fabric, blackened cloud-garments, sheltering by the hopeful
She unfolds herself just enough to grasp at cloud-drifts
Vacillating from earth to sky in soft-touch respite precipitations
Moistening and loosening women, toad-women, grouse-women, sky-
women
Women folded-over with late-summer bouquets scented of exhausted
wildflowers
Women heavy with voice.

KICKING AND SCREAMING

Babiigomakakiianskwe Dibaajim

Conversation with Toad Woman

I'm going to tell you a story that starts when I was a child. I don't like to do that, because it lets people think that contemporary Indians are just an adjunct to the past, that older Indian stuff is more cool than contemporary Indian stuff, and that maybe we have no place in this world other than as symbols of the past. But I'm going to start the story that way anyhow, because over the years, I've learned to start contemporary conversations by validating myself through the past.

OK, when I was a kid . . . we ate a lot of little stuff, like small perch, turtles, grouse, frogs' legs, wild mushrooms, and blackberries. There were a lot of us in my family, and we had time to take advantage of the fact that we occupied a large space—hundreds of acres of trees, lakes, ponds, swamps, open meadows, hayfields, and orchards. I am lucky, I guess, because we lived in a place where the interstate highway system took its time finishing itself and making an impact upon our world. When opportunities to improve our state of well-being took us northward, we stayed in remote family bush camps that allowed us to wrap ourselves around Lake Superior and its northernmost watershed peripheries. We unabashedly stood on the shore to watch moose dive underwater, and we leaned out from quiet canoes to let beavers and otters snuffle at our fingertips. We were followed by curious minks as we giggled our way along berry-picking trails. We were hidden in abundance.

We had an intimacy with our food sources. We actually procured and killed the things we ate. We also apologized to each creature for taking its life to sustain our own. We were aware of our roles as predators in the local food chain, and we were grateful to be at the top, even if comfort was a constant effort.

There was on our farm, back then, a children's tractor, and it was used to keep my siblings, cousins, and me productive, out of trouble, and occupied such that we didn't ask our parents for anything they couldn't provide. We used it to haul logs for firewood, one at a time;

and we used it to ride miles and miles to town to buy and eat ice cream once a week throughout the summer. I didn't know anything about horsepower back then, and never dreamed that I'd ever own a John Deere 95-horsepower four-wheel drive tractor with tires taller than a man, so I can't tell you how many workhorses the old Massey Ferguson was equivalent to. I'm guessing maybe one and a half, because that's more than well-trained children really needed.

That Fergie had two tires, but it pulled a two-wheeled wooden cart behind it, so it was as well-balanced as any four-wheeled tractor or modern marvel. The cart had a two-by-six cedar board bolted across its top near the front; and the hard springing board served as the driver's seat. The Fergie was a very old tractor, its rust indistinguishable from its muted red history; and it had a hinged metal glove box to the far right above the engine. The glove box actually held work gloves, as well as a wrench . . . But the oldest child living at home, the responsibility-laden driver of the tractor, was the only one who was ever taught what to do with the wrench (adjust the idle). In addition to the heavy leather gloves and the mysterious wrench, the glove box also held a couple of feet of small-gauge rope with a pull-handle at one end. The pull-handle was a piece of wood about four or five inches long that was connected to a rope and, when pulled, engaged a flywheel. The flywheel on the tractor was on one side of the engine, and the rope was wrapped around it and then yanked to start the engine. There was no key, no battery, no electric start. That's why I keep thinking this tractor was only equivalent to about one and a half horses, because a child could start it with a short rope on a flywheel. It was, of course, a great honor to pull that flywheel's starter rope. All of us got a turn sooner or later, and the older-child drivers were always well-trained to be patient with small ones who wrapped and yanked the rope over and over until the tractor started . . . or didn't. A battery might run out of energy, but, back then, children were endless renewable resources. We were pumpers of hand pumps, haulers of firewood, and pluckers of wild fruits.

My most vivid memories of that tractor are of being a passenger while an older child, a young uncle, silently drove us to and from work and play. He was kind and patient and always had a smile on his face. I can say from personal experience that it was hard not to smile while driving the old Fergie. I grew into that honor myself. But this particular older child was a smiler; and after he grew up and bought himself an old Model-T, I remember him smiling, still, looking back and comically arching his eyebrows while we rode in the rumble seat. I don't remember the Model-T going much beyond the boundaries of the children's tractor, though. I guess our farm world held enough fields, woods, and dirt roads to fill up our childhoods.

The tractor was how we got to and from the school bus stop, which was about a mile and a half from our house. We hid the tractor in the woods before standing and waiting at a road intersection for the school bus, making it look for all the world like we'd walked the whole way there and hadn't been enjoying ourselves. The first quarter mile of the trip was uphill, because our house was close to shallow water, where my father had hand-pounded our well. The rest of the trip toward civilization was mostly on a flat. But, believe me, we knew every rise and dip along the way. When the tractor was out of commission, we walked uphill. When the tractor was working, we cut the engine and flew down the shallowest of the downhill slopes. In neutral, Fergie sang out a metallic *click, click, click, click.* One punched on the clutch and shifted gears to start up the engine mid-roll, throwing us all into a lurch right before the next rise in the road.

Of course, I need to mention that the tractor's only brake was a metal bar with a flap of rubber at the bottom, which the driver dragged in the dirt to slow down the momentum of the engine and its load— which was frequently at least a half dozen children, and sometimes as many as a dozen or more. I remember when I came to the point in my life where I was allowed to be a driver . . . and I can tell you that the paucity of power in that brake came as a shock. The only way to stop the thing by pulling the brake was to yell to the rest of the kids to hop off the back of the rear cart, to lessen the forward energy and the weight I had to work against. I learned to use the lower gear to come downhill toward the house and to aim for an uphill slope when I planned a stop.

I remember how sometimes my young uncle would turn around, put a finger to his lips, then pull over to the shoulder of the dirt road and wrap his whole lean body around the brake bar. It took me decades to learn enough about hunting grouse to understand why he knew what to do, but he'd always been observing the grouse as they flew across our path. (The rest of us were too little to care.) When the tractor was stopped near a grouse-rising, heavy gloves were removed from the glove box. I don't remember at what point I was trained to help with the hunt, because I don't ever remember not knowing what we were doing when we stopped. No one had to be given verbal directions. We silently slipped from the back of the cart and followed the older boy's hand signals. We made a large circle. Then we walked slowly, carefully, in toward him. When the diameter of our circle was just small enough that the height of our bodies blocked the grouse's exit, he would reach down and grab that grouse with both gloved hands. It was a thing of beauty. He snapped the neck and we admired our prize all the way home. There was gold in the feathers, softness to be pressed against our faces, and the fading warmth of a life sacrificed for our own nutrition.

Cleaning the grouse was light work. I've seen people just skin a grouse and quickly sauté only the breasts and legs. But there were so many of us that we plucked the whole thing, so we had feathers to blow about and something like a small chicken to stuff and bake. Usually we waited until we had more than one. We used that tractor for gathering small bits of food—sometimes only blackberries along the sunshine of that dirt road—but with so many of us, enough to make at least one pie, usually two. Don't let me get started on blueberries . . . because the point I want to make, to wander back into the present eventually, is to talk about gathering food. And the rest of this story doesn't have anything to do with the kids' tractor.

There were a lot of us—fifteen children, siblings and cousins to one another, between the two families. Add to that visiting relatives and sleepover best friends, and there were enough of us for two opposing baseball teams, although the makeup of the teams varied from day to day, and there were no "official" teams. In fact, we had no concept of teams; we'd rarely seen television, and we didn't know much about commercial sports or rivalry between static, locality-based opposing teams. We only knew that there were supposed to be eight people on each side, to make it fair, so we could have a good, drawn-out baseball game to fill up a few free hours. We didn't even grasp the concept of one side or another's beating the other. There wasn't much of a concept of superiority in all of it. If one team was short a person, we swapped a smaller player for an older one. No one burst into tears or stomped off. We balanced out everything, so that games lasted longer and supplied us with more enjoyment.

We played around with wooden baseball bats back then, winging them at just about everything in sight—and they were wonderful things. New, smooth baseball bats were only used with baseballs, and the older baseball bats were used for everything else. Of course, they were used to hit rocks into the lakes, which made them too battered to reliably steer a baseball. You'd throw a rock up into the air, hike the bat over a shoulder, wait for the descent, swing, and *zzzzziiiiinnngg* . . . It made your arms buzz right up to the larynx. We usually picked white stones for batting into the lake, because baseballs were white, and we were practicing for hitting the ball. Of course, this made us all into wicked-good hitters, because hitting a rock was a whole lot harder than hitting a big ol' softball. So the baseball games that filled the space between our two cousin households were pretty amazing, and kids from the school in town never much wanted to play with us. Most of us could swing and hit a gnat.

So now you might finally understand that there were a lot of us, and that, for the most part, we cooperated all day and all night to make things work, to keep ourselves occupied, fed, and happy. You see part of the rest of this story is about food, about procuring things—small things—because we were small people, and small things were what we did best . . . like mushrooms, for stringing to dry behind the woodstove, where they became so small and fragrant.

OK, so now I can talk about bullfrogs, because we ate frogs' legs. There wasn't much else on the frogs big enough to eat. They had lean frames, those frogs, with big, fleshy legs for flipping those froggie-frames this way and that, for chasing after minnows and insects, and for escaping from predators (like us). I think I told you that we were predators, too. And because there were so many of us, we were efficient predators of small things. We loved frogs' legs. They were as good as the potato chips you could buy at a gas station. But I don't recall going to a gas station much as a kid because we had an underground, hand-pump gas tank on the farm, and we just took turns pumping away, rain or shine. Eventually we pumped our way to the crispiness of the fins and tails of small fish and of the webbed hind feet of frogs when they are fried up for the satisfaction of children. Those small things were glorious delicacies.

So this story isn't about baseball or tractors. It's about when we would supplement a fish fry with other small life forms. And we ate fried fish at least once a week. We had very strict rules in our family about distribution of the fish fins and tails and the webbed feet of the frogs' legs because they were rich in calcium and full of cartilage; tiny bones that gave a satisfying crunch and then melted in the mouth. We had all the big fish we wanted, but everybody loved the little ones best. And everybody loved frogs' legs. Everybody got at least one. So, when we knew we were going to fry up panfish, maybe with a few bullheads, bass, or pike, we always hunted for bullfrogs, too. We lived on hundreds of acres, and we were only a few dozen people along miles of water-front hunting grounds. The hunting wasn't just for food. Like the kids' tractor, it was childcare; and it was an education in environmental activism. We kept track of where we harvested, and we tried not to overharvest or to spend too much time in places where various species needed to live and reproduce. We gave them their space. And we thanked them for giving their lives to feed us. We prayed out loud that way. We prayed every day. We prayed to be good caretakers and responsible for the fish and the frogs.

We selectively gathered from the resources around us, including frogs. Sometimes we went out in the dark, with handmade torches or electric flashlights. We walked barefoot in the mucky shallows of the lakes, seeps, and ponds. There weren't many broken bottles or razor-sharp beer cans for us to worry about stepping on. Our world hadn't been discovered yet. Commercial recycling wasn't yet available, but we lived in a world where those things were controlled, and if not repurposed, deposited far away from areas where we lived and played. We preserved most of our food in canning jars, so we didn't generate much trash.

We moved together like one single organism, finding comfort in one another's presence, teasing, poking, grasping at the loose fabric of one another's wool sweaters while we stumbled along dark, familiar shorelines. We'd thrust our small lights forward, and as one of us came upon an exceptionally large bullfrog, frozen, immobile in the light, a partner swung down with a baseball bat, then a third child stabbed the stunned animal with a sharpened stick or a pocket knife or just grabbed it. Other times we simply watched the sunlight and shadows and ambushed a few bullfrogs in broad daylight. I don't remember ever being taught about when a frog was too small to harvest so that there would always be a steady supply. It was something I always knew. I didn't know how to think otherwise. None of us knew how to live and think any other way than to plan for the future.

Now, I suppose it is time to bring this story into the present, because it is about a toad, a large toad, large enough to harvest its legs, were it a frog—which was the first thing that came to my mind when I saw it. Most days now, I don't have access to hundreds of acres of land and miles of borderland between water and terra firma. Those things have become the domain of a socioeconomic class that is beyond most of those children of my childhood stories. Where I live today, those habitats are now full of big unnatural things, like waterfront mansions rather than small creatures. So I sit here on a dry hilltop, and I marvel that I share my world with a few small frogs and even a few large toads.

Frogs and toads don't sip water. They absorb water through their skin. And they do pretty well, as long as there are small ponds nearby or hollow tree trunks full of rainwater, or heavy, life-giving dew. But lately summers here have extended periods of dry, dewless mornings, and I've begun to wonder if frogs and toads, too, mourn their loss of opportunities for comfort and survival. Is a brown toad much different from a brown woman? Should we be reaching out to one another for survival and verbal exchange?

This is perhaps the point in this story where many people's sympathetic leanings toward wildlife habitat protection might kick in. After all, we're discovering that amphibians are canaries in the coal mines, so to speak, in terms of the health of our environment. And perhaps it is time to assess and control our inroads into the territories formerly occupied by indigenous peoples so that we can save frogs and toads. Lord knows they are gentle and harmless members of their respective ecosystems and cultures, and they deserve our empathy and protection.

I also worry a little that the domain of environmental stewardship is, these days, dominated by a socioeconomic elite that leaves me out of the formula.

And this probably isn't the point in the story where I should start talking about how people of color might actually be valuable members of our own respective ecosystems, deserving of empathy and protection, too. But I grew up being taught by my family that I was an important part of my environment, and that I deserved to be here and to be protected. (For what it's worth, I need to mention this: Many people who, for the most part, are willing to pool their resources to help ensure the survival of frogs and toads would probably not be concerned about the survival of defenseless brown children who are regularly assaulted and tossed aside by exclusionary institutionalized otherness.)

Which brings us back to the main character in this story—the brown toad.

The first time I saw the toad, I'd just come home from the grocery store in Traverse City. I'd gone to town as early as possible to take advantage of morning's coolness. As I carried groceries from the car to the house, I noticed that what appeared to be a large brown leaf had landed in the pets' water dish. I bent to scoop it out so that it would not add tannin to the water. But I saw that the brown object was a beautiful bug-eating friend, and I pulled back my hand. I distracted the pets, hurried in with the groceries, and gave the toad her personal space.

I could shoo her away any time I want to, but our relationship is not about my survival or satisfaction anymore. It's about the toad's survival. Now, I have a separate water dish around the corner of the house where grass grows long, and Toad Woman remains undisturbed by pets and perceived predators. Toad Woman has taken to using that bowl exclusively as her own, and I clean it daily, refilling it with rainwater or well water that is free of additives and toad poop.

I've started talking to her a lot lately, and I wonder if she feels that I belong to her, like a large, semi-predictable pet. We discuss a lot of taboo topics, such as racism and socioeconomic exclusion. And I feel pretty safe talking to her about these things, because we are able to keep our opinions within the small circle of the water dishes, where we won't offend anybody or cause a backlash. While I sip my second or third cup of coffee, she rehydrates, and the contents of her intestines swell. I excuse myself to get on with my day, and later I will empty her bowel movement onto precious medicine plants I keep near my doorstep. I nurture them with rainwater, and these days I let a bit of that water pass through my friend before nurturing my soul with the old plants and memories of our usefulness. Neither of us has to risk retaliation by sharing our experiences with the outside world. It's an odd relationship with the rest of the world that we've carved out for ourselves, not unlike the way Indian authors tend to write their most talking-back pieces for Indian audiences. Toad Woman stays hidden around the corner, accessing fresh water in a world of invisibility. Native American scholars, and women of color in general, live in small, "safe," underfunded pockets of the academy and the workforce while absorbing and gleaning what is deemed acceptable by something bigger and more powerful than us. Functioning from around the corner makes us think creatively, to find satisfaction and competence in small achievements, such as the recycling of toad feces.

I suppose that brings me back to the subject of the past versus the present, because my survival, in terms of who I am, culturally and personally, is dependent upon memories and hope. I am intertwined with changes in access to resources, as is the toad. Cultural survival is not just pitted against changes in resources, but against the loss of respect for those resources. I remember my place in the ecosystem as being one of cognizance, of competence. I don't remember being a relic. I don't remember existing as an Indian in nature just for the entertainment of others or for the preservation of stories. I remember being an environmental steward, *part* of my environment, because we *depended* upon that environment. I remember learning that *we* are the stories, and that the stories are fluid to meet our changing cultural and individual needs. That is why it is very important to me that I not let anybody get confused about my status as a placeholder for stereotypes versus my role as a leader, a teacher, a scientist, or a conservationist. I need to make sure that people understand that I am as valuable today as I was a hundred years or more ago. Just ask Toad Woman. Maybe from around the corner, she'll sing you a contemporary/traditional song about resilience and strength.

SING THIS SNOWFALL LIKE A MEMORY

It was bound to happen, eventually . . .
After all those ice ages,
After the sun kept rising and setting in the same general directions
While the landscape turned and shaped itself
Under his predictability,
And his offspring became overdependent and too vocal . . .
(Even the coyotes had fallen in love with the sounds of their own
voices.)

One day the West Wind couldn't handle the responsibility anymore.
He got tired and started drinking every night after work.
He grew a big beer belly,
Ignored his wife and children,
Became forgetful with his paycheck,
Leaving it under a sickly ash tree,
Where he'd fallen asleep counting the dead branches,
Waiting desperately for them to fall on their own.

He'd told the North Wind to leave him alone . . .
Unless he wanted to drive to town for a six pack,
Or had a pint in his glove box,
Maybe found a smoked chub thick with salt,
Or wanted to go ice fishing for bluegills
On a frozen lake, downhill from the highway,
Upwind from change and monuments impervious to blasting sands.

Insects had bored into his chest,
Tearing away at his arteries and clogging them with asphalt
Under outdoor floodlights
Because their larvae were afraid of sunset
And the denseness of standing trees

Thick with life and droppings from his offspring
Who chewed twigs for a living and barked at night breezes.

When his bones hurt, he'd grow angry
From the burden of constant responsibility . . .
And he'd throw hailstones at his dogs;
Or he'd cry and lean in heavily toward empathy,
Gently smothering a soft grouse under a blanket of snow
To save it from a painful death by broken wing
Or loss of leeway in a world of predation.

But some days he just stopped caring . . .
So old Biboon would creep in for mischief,
Dropping snows in straight deadfalls,
Mastering gravity in thick sheets
Of heavy and wet,
While Time held her breath and watched in amazement
Until he reached deep into her pockets for pufflets from the east.

Some days, the West Wind slumped in a stupor next to his
woodstove . . .
And opportunistic clouds drifted in, full of darkness,
Full of moisture,
Full of waiting,
Full of need,
And they opened up their overcoats,
Dumping small white birds from the sky like rain.

One day, he pushed his oldest son out onto a frozen lake,
Where he taunted the boy until he danced so hard
That he broke up the ice
And left pockets of cold, open water
To lure eagles in search of resilient winter ducks.
But they were only decoys shaped out of ice
So that underwater cougars could pull them to their death.

His wife and children wove blankets
Of boiled thistles intertwined with strips of rabbit fur,
White, like lifesaving snowbanks
Where they hid, like warriors eluding rival fur traders,
In their desperation to weave continuity
And predictability
Into a world of fatigue.

His mother-in-law made him hot teas
Out of *mashkiginiibishan,*
And the heathers flowed through his nostrils
Like songs from his childhood.
He slept for a month,
Undisturbed
By the hungry bedside cries of ravens and children.

When he woke up, we wrapped ourselves in porcupine quills
And danced in warm, close circles.
Then we ran outside, laughing, and scattered over frozen lakes like
leftover pollen.

A Song for Anny

Up in the Sault,
There's an old lady,
Maybe not so old, but old enough
That she holds wisps of old winds between her fingers
And songs that she had almost been tempted
To let go of
When breezes wrapped around the equinox
Escalated into screaming windstorms
With snagged bits of mink flesh
Dangling between their shiny, ragged teeth,
Up and down the coastlines,
Where gulls stopped screaming,
Gagging on ships' ballasts,
And almost fooled crows into taking the quiet for granted.

You can bring her bundles of tobacco,
Wrapped in calico
Made from old milk jugs
Recycled into hopes for the future;
And it can even be the kind of tobacco
Sold in Reservation gas stations
Up front by the door
Where you can't miss it,
And there's a picture of a plains warrior
In full headdress,
Printed in red,
So you can't mistake the association
For something less than the marketing of death
To wannabe warriors
On asphalt highways to no place in particular,
Or maybe to a small diesel fishing tug,
Where boys can feel like strongmen.

And that old lady,
She'll take that poisoned tobacco
Bred full of addiction,
Look past its history of exploitation,
And she'll take it in the spirit in which it is given,
As an alias for tradition.
Then she'll pull apart her long graying braid
And untangle long strands of sweetgrass,
Fine, flexible roots from streambed red willows,
Giishik,
Miskiwiimin aniibiishan,
Aandeg bagoosan;
And she'll stir these things together
In a cast-iron skillet
Over hot rocks,
Behind the casino,
Where she taught young men
How to build sweat lodges
Out of sheet plastic.

And just when you think
That you've got jangling gambling chips
In your pocket,
She'll let pufflets of past winds
Slip out of her fingers,
Across your forehead,
Scenting your hair gel
With fresh spawn from lake trout
And ground up powders
From fragrant sumacs
That shouted jagged songs at you
From mounded roadsides,
Before you knew how to sit quietly
And listen
For old ravens coughing up

Rhythms like the snapping of twigs
During heavy, wet snowfalls.

If you bundle up these things,
Carefully,
With prayers on your fingertips,
She will tell you a story
About the Indian guy
Who used to deliver the U.S. mail by dogsled,
In and out of the treelines,
Delivering news
About the conditions of the ice
On the lakes and ponds
That wrapped themselves around Turtle Island,
Weaving trails and maplines
For pow wows
And prayers,
For good times and survival,
Trade goods and Indian baskets,
Dried berries and love songs,
Engine oil and *skwataagin,*
All stitched up in careful bundles,
Insulated with cattail fibers
And fur from old dogs to whom he still sang loving songs.

He left the post office before sunup,
With smiles and songs about ice crystals
Tucked into his pockets;
And they would slip out
At every wind-battered household,
Where he delivered tax bills
Coiled inside of birch bark cylinders,
Smooth with quilled symmetrical rosebuds;
Letters from pileated woodpeckers who had fled to the city
For jobs in the ironworks
Or companionship in wood-sided pubs

With moose heads mounted over the polyester-painted tables
And pennies counter-sunk into wide holes
Drilled into their pine board histories;
Dried powders pounded from the spines of sturgeons
Who mailed home their own flesh
To thank their parents for
Keeping fires burning
Deep under their breastbones.

At every house on his postal route
He stopped for warm teas,
Dipped from tall pots
At the back of wood-burning cook stoves,
Where tired, old knees
Baked themselves into breads
Sweetened with tree saps
Boiled hard into solid hopes and dreams.
He nibbled on strips of dried pumpkin,
Dipped in thick syrups
That tasted like wood smoke,
Thick, and filling his nostrils
With prayers and drumbeats,
And small children bouncing
Up and down to the consistent rhythms of dark, close cabin walls
Full with familiar voicebeats.

After work each weekday,
He sang fresh songs to his dogs,
And they sledded up the coast to Gros Cap,
Where he ran gill nets under the ice,
Threaded on long poles
Made of poplar saplings
That he trimmed smooth
With a favorite old pocketknife
Made from a shinbone
Pulled from his own flesh,

From the cousin who exploded next to him
In an inland trench,
Just past Normandy,
Where Anishinaabe boys signed up
To prove their allegiance
To the American flag
And their determination
To become something more than Indian boys
In a time and place
Where hope seemed impossible.

That old lady
Will pull out that pocketknife
From a fold in her heavy skirt,
And she will whittle away
At the red willow roots
That held her graying braid
In place over her heartbeat,
And she will fill her pipe
With determination
That she will light with a tinder
Chipped from her own forearm;
Then the room will become thick
With sweet smokes and vapors
That soften your lungs
Into gentle songs
About your own childhood,
While you blink into white mists
That smell like fried venison steaks,
Midmorning,
Between ice ages.

If you pry open the *wiigob* fibers
Wrapped around your own chest,
She will open up a basswood pouch
Full of coarse salt

That you can sprinkle on your roasted corn.
The kernels are so small
That they fit between the songbeats
That pound across the parking lot from the casino,
Where the plastic chips clink in rhythm
To the cries of snowmobiles
Up and down old Shunk Road,
Past the ghosts of Shedawinag
Smiling upward
From mounds they built
Out of clay from streambeds
That flowed with their own blood.

She will unfold long mats
Made from shallow-water reeds
Stitched together wide end to narrow end,
From one shoreline to another;
And she will instruct you
How to hang them over the saplings
Against the sheet plastic,
To keep out acid winds from I-75,
A crow's line of beating cylinders
Drumming out exhaust songs
All the way to the Canadian border,
Where dashes and dots
Emulate the love songs of whitefish
Flashing up the rapids,
Reading day lengths like roadmaps
Into the uppermost basins
Of perseverance.

If you crawl over the ice
On your belly
Underneath the cliff
Where the Agawaa boys
Set their gill nets,

And you let Michiibizhiw gnaw
At the Thunderbird
You had tattooed on the small of your back
When cold beers helped you forget
The lake swells that threw your small fishing tug
Toward rock reefs between islands,
She will pat your dried symbolism
Into her pipe bowl
And puff
Until your eyes water,
And you spread your wings
To circle above the smoke hole
Into clear currents
Above the foray,
Where you can glide upside down
And lock talons with other ambitious young Thunderbirds,
Practicing how to fly
And protect your territory.

Desperation Cookies

Old Angie, you stand in line outside the food bank
Before the door jack is kicked away by people who are tired of taking
care of you.
You take a number from the roulette wheel ticket dispenser,
And you sit on a soft chair next to the disenfranchised migrant
Who stole the peaches you were planning to can from your last peach
tree,
Right after he was given your job at the plant where your diploma
gathered dust.

When the lady with the clipboard offers you bruised peaches,
You decide not to cry and take two broken bananas instead.

A woman in a gown spins the wheel, and you get to choose
Between two small cans of beans or one big bag of dried.
You choose dried when you have electricity to cook them,
Canned, when you don't.

Smile, when you remember how you once had a wood-burning
cookstove,
And wild peas grew from pink flowers all around you, Angie.

At the shelf of canned green beans, you ponder how you will use
them
With the quarts of wax beans you put away four years ago
When you still had access to rainfall.
If you say, *no, thank you,* you will seem ungrateful.
Pick the macaroni, Angie, pick the macaroni.

I'll take a living wage, please.
You can't buy a vowel, Angie. We only have macaroni and cheese.

Old Angie, you hear the roulette wheel whirring over and over,
And you try to keep up with the chicken noodle or bean 'n' bacon,
And the saltines keep coming, like elevator music on a wet day.
The tuna cans will serve well as hockey pucks, if someone comes to visit,
Because you have lake trout pumping through your veins.

Old Angie, don't be afraid to look up from the paper bags where you rearrange your self-respect
And wait for the laundry soap to appear from around the corner.

Oatmeal or cereal? OATMEAL OR CEREAL??? (There is no one in line behind you.)
OATMEAL OR CEREAL??? I'll take a job, please.
OATMEAL OR CEREAL??? What's wrong with you? Decide—quick.
Cereal, yes, cereal. Cereal, yes. Surreal, yes. Surreal.
You used to own the watershed, and now you crawl into town for groceries on four cylinders.

I'll take just one can of opportunity, please.
You can't pick a consonant, Angie, but we've got *whole wheat* spaghetti today.

It's OK to fantasize about eating Crispy Oat Loops with wild raspberries,
Or maybe a fresh luncheon salad of Crispy Oat Loops with lake trout and watercress
Or a venison tenderloin.
Before you start to laugh, remember the bag of chocolate chips you might have in the cupboard
From the last time you had a day of hard work;
Then go home and celebrate the jar of olives that was on the "extra" shelf.

You can breathe again when you get back out into the parking lot, Angie.
In the waiting room, I saw cloudbanks break apart when you looked up from your *National Geographic.*

Old Angie, I promise to come to your house for desperation cookies
After you write yourself a love song about hunting caribou with your mother.
I will pour cold coffee over the rough spot in your ice rink
And scatter table salt over your driveway to make it safe.
Melt the chocolate with peanuts and hope, and I will watch you stir in the cereal, over and over and over, until it tastes like competence.

CRANBERRY-PICKING SEASON

Folded-Over Woman missed cranberry-picking season this year,
Because she was cradling mountains in her arms,
Rocking them gently against her bosom until they slept,
And dustings of snow could fall quietly upon their jagged young
peaks and reddened cheeks.

They shuddered and rested until spring's melts,
When rivulets ran between her breasts,
Along the rises and dips of her ribcage and belly,
Finally cascading between her thighs.

They would wake to thunder and wail like windstorms,
While the warmth of her body shed into streams and rivers,
With anxious canyons and carefree rapids echoing through her
springtimes,
Her long breasts stretching downward to nurse wildfowl and
ruminants.

Folded-Over Woman watched over her offspring who survived the
long winters,
Her joints growing thin, splintering off, bones shattering like
limestone,
While antlered snakes crept through crevices beneath her feet,
Causing her stone-cast nurseries to shake and crumble.

Folded-Over Woman missed cranberry-picking season this year,
Because she was working in a day care center,
Soaking illness and poverty into her long arms and lungs
While she wished away wasted years of foreign education and
underemployment.

She breathed heavy and dry, coughing up mountaintops and snowmelt,
While health care and opportunity flushed through her treetops,
Swept past her chilled arteries and internal bedrock,
Gushed past her like transport trucks on a hardened highway to never.

She would quiver and roll onto a mounded side,
Resting until winter's dull respite,
While overheated mountains rumbled into her kitchen and cried out for nurturing
And her long breasts stretched downward to nurse habitats for generations.

Folded-Over Woman healed herself in scaled-bark patchwork,
Retreating into her own bosom during summer's solstice,
Waiting for fresh breezes and new, broad eyes and ears
To listen for hope and survival until the next season of autumn's cranberries.

Folded-Over Woman missed cranberry-picking season this year,
Because she was working in a nursing home,
Where she was scorned and screeched at by a young beetle with half her credentials,
And she cried on the roadside where she picked wildflowers for her bedridden elders.

They shuddered and slid their fingers through the boughs of her long hair,
While their autumns progressed, their own children heaved westward,
And their limbs ached with pride in gashes of longevity,
Her long breasts stretching downward to nurse the desperate and helpless.

She would hold them to her warm body and soft nourishing heartbeat,

Where they would crumble into soft clays and valleys of gravel,
Lifetimes of their snows tumbling down her crevices,
Willing boulders to her valleys, rounding youth into experience.

Folded-Over Woman sheltered their lifetimes,
Caressed their aspirations and accomplishments,
Ran her palms along their stiffened branches and sentiments,
And massaged their ancient secrets into histories and stories of
success.

Folded-Over Woman missed cranberry-picking season this year,
Because drills and hydraulic internal parasites shoved themselves hard
and unlubricated
Into the wet sands beneath her hearth,
Causing her hand-hewn floorboards to buckle at their strongest
foundation points.

She tried tucking a matchbook under a cast-iron foot of her
cookstove,
While its brittle iron teetered and shrieked
And searched for bedrock,
While she shoved a wider wedge of cedar into the emptiness.

She would reach for ancient volcanic glass as it stretched at her
windowpanes,
Shuddered, and cut into her flesh like an injured dog,
Her life lessons seeping into the floorboards,
Useless in place and time, modern expectations, and economics.

Folded-Over Woman folded deeper into herself,
Holding overworked generations in her arms,
Agate eyes scanning her horizons for mountaintops to nurture,
As her breasts stretched downward and hardened into ropes of cold
lava.

Folded-Over Woman filled her buckets with wild cranberries this
season,
Unfolding torn muscles briefly between seasons of heat and hardness,
Between advancing cold and autumn's warm dip into the space
between her soft breasts,
Where she cradled young mountains in her arms and gently rocked
them into quiet sleep.

I LEFT A MAP THROUGH THE DIASPORA

Just in case you forget where I left my love songs,
I buried them in shallow, sandy soils
Under a searing forest fire that raged
From east to west, fueled by prevailing winds.

There is a little piece of one
Shoved into a rotted-out knothole
At the confluence of two jack pines,
Whittled into a soup bowl by an insistent sapsucker.

There is a map to the next one
Hidden under the long oval feces of porcupines
At the base of a den tree,
Where dogs begin barking and snapping every dawn until the sun
forfeits.

I shoved one onto the tongue
Of a doe struck down by a transport truck
On the highway behind our old shorelines,
Where even hungry eagles sought out new sources of rotting flesh.

I'm certain that I tied a small, tattered strip of one
To a branch of a mountain ash
That was broken down by an angry, adolescent bear
During a season of drought and desperation.

I tattooed one on my shoulder blade
Just underneath the skin,
Using ice crystals for needles
And black spruce ashes for dark inks to contrast against my fears.

There are some backbeats and foolish rhymes
Woven into net weights made from clamshells
That pound themselves into bits of calcium
For the balancing stones inside of fishes' skulls.

There is a love song covered in gravel
In the highest inland-facing cave
Midway up the cliff, *mijiinadoon minisaabikong,*
Wrapped in an amniotic sac and hidden inside cambium birch bark.

I scribbled one in red ochres
At the base of the cliff
Where we sifted agates out of crumbling conglomerate
And strung them around our necks on long cedar twines.

I tucked one between the floorboards
During the last windstorm
In the hopes that the weather would turn,
And we could find respite from sharp crystals of ragged frost.

I tied some to boulders
And threw them over the cliff
Where the Black River empties into Lake Superior,
Weighted down forever against determined currents.

The first stanzas of one song
Are enclosed in faint embers
That I placed along the breastbones of dying waterfowl,
Praying that each one would miraculously soar.

I threw the rest of them
Into the spray made by hard waves pounding volcanic rocks
In the hopes that they would rise up
To find bits of floating hope with which their electrons might
intertwine.

I thought I heard one
Whispering back at me through thick nights
When I looked up from sorting beechnuts,
Listening for the wind to soften.

Biboon Was a Friend of Mine

I used to save big buttons from old woolen coats,
And I would string them into bull-roarers for the old man.
He would twirl them between his armlengths and his chin,
Calling in windstorms from the four directions
With loud, heavy roaring demands from a child's simple toy.
He even smiled when he did it.

He used to make rasps out of pithy lake reeds,
And he'd *tap, tap, tap* them over hollow logs for small children,
Teaching them how to smile and hum at the same time.
Ducks would *sheeb, sheeb, sheeb* to the soundsource,
And he'd throw them bits of his breakfast, like songs on a breeze.

Before the lake ice became too thin,
He used to sled away out to the big islands for days,
Returning with mink in his pockets and a pouch full of stories
That he poured over suppers like gravy,
Scattering the leftovers into the clouds at sunset.

For a while, he went south for a job in the steel mill,
Where he saved up enough money to buy a snow machine;
And I heard that the old man snuck back into Sault Ste. Marie at night
with his dogs,
Picking up frozen grouse all along the concrete-block foundations of
houses,
Where the birds had mistaken reflections for nothingness between
trees
And pushed their skulls into plate glass.
He had a frying pan made of bedrock
In which he quickly sautéed his finds in melted snow
And served them up with potatoes and fleeting glances.

Some days he used a bullroarer to part the skies
So that he could lie still on a cobble beach in the sunshine,
Tapping together pebbles in rhythms between his naps;
And caribou would appear from the gray trunks of balsams
To sniff at the hollow part of his ear.

I would laugh out loud and shout out an old song in his direction,
Then turn back to my quillwork to finish a pull.
And when I looked up again, they were both gone,
The old man and the caribou.
And I had nothing left but the bull-roarers and the songs
He had been singing to me since I was a child.

THE LAST CARIBOU

I remember that there was a strong piebald gene in the herd,
And that I knew them, each one,
The older, experienced ones that snorted and shook their antlers
When younger ones like you boasted and stamped their feet . . .

I watched calves shiver as their amniotic sacks were licked away,
Exposing them to lakeside breezes
Chilled by basins of snowmelts
Whose density and volume protected them from determined
predators.

I watched them dance and sing and pray
Every time a new calf took a first step
Or swam after a parent from one small island to the next,
Clambering upward and mastering bedrock.

I listened to them sing gray and white piebald songs of joy
With the coming of seasons, the coming of rut,
The lushness of grass, the rare birth of twins,
Splashing with joy in cold, fresh snowmelts.

I heard rumors that most of the rest of the herd moved out to some
wide, flat islands down the coast,
All except the piebalds,
Reclusive and uncomfortable with their otherness.
They found comfort in familiar sounds and smells in their home
coves and islands.

When I listened with my own heartbeat, I could hear the piebalds
singing,
Their leg tendons snapping out rhythms as they blended into spruce
trunks

And skittered pebbles across cobble beaches
From one antlered trail to the next.

Younger males had headed south to Babiigwaadina'a to seek their fortunes
Where intruders were afraid to stay
Because of the power of the river:
Twisting beach sands at the base of steep, narrow ravines and crushing waters.

They grew into large, strong caribou families,
Their campfires brightening the shoreline
As they steeped lichens into breakfast teas
And wove sleeping mats out of their own hollow chest hairs.

Their songs echoed up and down the coastline
With lessons about patches of green grass and how to outrun fishers.
They swam together in long lines like geese,
And they played stickball on the beaches with copper boulders.

Then, one year there was a brief period of winter respite from overheating waters . . .
When the big lake froze solid, white, and flat, as it did in my childhood,
For the first time in generations,
Confounding short-lived caribou and their inexperienced leaders.

Scientists sing in songs that the rest of the herd is gone now,
Misled by brief respite in changing climates and environments,
Followed out on the ice by packs of hungry wolves, busy being wolves,
Their fates packed away in museums with caches of caribou bones and burial bowls.

Back home, the piebalds lived business as usual,
Succumbing to predation, crying out in loneliness,

Praying out loud in desperation, with no new generations
To come home and renew their songs and stories with changing
histories and lessons.

I remember the last female piebald,
Old and persistent, lean and hardworking.
She began darting across open beaches, looking back over her
shoulder,
Sliding into dark gray spruce bark, disguising her piebald as a bright
patch of birch.

I had seen her at ice-out, calm and singing grazing songs,
Followed across lava beds by last year's calf,
A sign that she had not bred again,
And shared her days and nights with hope for tomorrows.

Then, somewhere between aspen blooms and wild yellow irises, the
calf disappeared;
And the cow bore only one antler weighing her down in a relentless
running tilt
As she searched the shorelines, wide-eyed and desperate,
Until she collapsed, exhausted, in the absorbing silt of a south-facing
bay.

I remember how ravens sang at her side for four days and cried rasps,
Until a red-tailed hawk spiraled down
And tore open the elegant spaces between her ribcage.
We all moved in and distributed her flesh on the hillsides.

Years ago, she had given birth to a daughter,
But, intimidated by the presence of predators and the precariousness
of her own piebald herd,
The daughter slowly transformed herself into a wolf
And eschewed her caribou heritage.

I remember how the girl-wolf had long, dark, lilting eyes.
But after some years, they were flecked with yellow,
And coarse hairs grew on the back of her neck.
I heard her growl and watched her caribou mother become sad, then afraid.

One spring I saw some fat piebald wolf pups
Sniffing around that birch stump where I saw you born,
Pushed out between pants and hard muscle slides;
But the pups all had yellow, unblinking eyes and turned away, uphill, to the business of being wolves.

I remember an old song about how the antlered ones had all been one clan,
Each filling a niche along the shores of the big lakes.
The song says that somewhere just north of Babiigwaadina'a,
Lake-fed snows grew too demanding for Deer Clan to walk among them,
And so, we changed our family name to Moose.

We grew long leg bones for dancing through deep snow,
Stepping quickly between the hearts of our loved ones,
Where we birthed stories about ourselves as giants
And taught our children songs about sharing the shorelines.

Before humans came along and built a dam, somewhere just south of Babiigwaadina'a,
I remember long pathways in and out of the old beach line,
Now scoured empty, deprived of the river's silts,
Where the footprints of caribou, deer, and moose were frozen in slush every spring morning,

Each cousin sharing the dance rhythms in turn,
Each browsing in a different place at a different hour,
Overlapping and sharing songs, stories, and lessons for their children
Under a single firelit canopy in one small, wet corner of the universe.

I don't recall any old songs about disappearing with the river silt,
So, forgive me if I sing about my family
Across wide-open waters, from between heavy spruce boughs.
I remember crying at sunrise with the last caribou.

GEOGRAPHIC ANALYSIS OF HEARTS AND LUNGS OF HOLOCAUST SURVIVORS

GEOGRAPHY

Somewhere outside of Minneapolis,
Where a soft prairie hill was scooped away to level a parking lot
Back behind the casino . . .
There is a long sandy ravine
That curls its way downward to the river that goes on forever.

Under desiccated roots of small, stranded jack pines,
West Wind and North Wind lean against opposing sandbanks.
Their knees are bent,
And their wide winter work boots rest flat against frozen clay.

The old blue enamel coffeepot is propped up over coals
By three glacial stones
As smooth as a loving woman's lips,
Each balanced in perfect harmony with the tilt of prairie demands
Upon curving soils and incessant winds.

West Wind suggests a smoke,
But North Wind says, no, better save the red willows
For making dream catchers to sell at pow wows,
. . . For making gas money to their next destination,
Where their extended families might be in need of a satisfying breeze.

West Wind and North Wind are playing three-handed pinochle with a
dummy hand,
Because the Anishinaabeg have been scattered about
So far in every direction,
Some even as far south as Oklahoma, says North Wind.

West Wind says he heard that the Kickapoo got to Oklahoma,
Then decided to keep going just across the border to Mexico,

Where brown Indian men and women fell in love with them
And wrapped their arms around them.

Now they build their wigwams out of red cedar
Instead of elm and birch barks;
They eat fatty seeds from cholla and rich pine nuts
Instead of beechnuts and hazelnuts from wide water basins.

The Kickapoo, who named themselves after lake-effect snows
At the southernmost tip of Lake Michigan's watershed,
Now dance in circles of desert sands.
They sing in a soft blend of Anishinaabemowin and Spanish, he says.

And the two old men snigger,
As they have never learned the European tongues that sound to them jumbled
Like waves tumbling boulders of ice
Into pebbles that melt away
Like change in old men's pockets.

North Wind has pneumonia, has had it for months.
His laughter morphs
Into wild fits and short gasps as he croups up sputum,
Turns his head toward Indiana steel mills,
Where prairies flatten into the southern basins of Great Lakes and waterways.

He'd been gifted the illness by a child in Traverse City
Who had stuffed a finger inside her congested nostril,
Then handed the old man a store-bought cookie
In lieu of opportunity.

One time, North Wind ambled out into a broad parking lot where
buffalo once grazed above twin bays in the wake of wildfires.
There, he sought out others who had been afflicted,

Asking for their remedies, like spare change
On the salty paved floors between grocery carts and rusted pickup
trucks.

He volunteered for recess duty at an elementary school
Where children's eyes weeped,
And their infected windpipes constricted to make them howl
Like coyotes filling a niche
Where wolf cubs once slid behind tall pines.

He peeked into a teacher's lounge
And smiled at a young Scandinavian,
Asked if she knew how to cure
Lack of access to fresh, cool air.

She told him to use his paid sick leave
To visit a physician
Who would cure him with expensive herbal teas from distant
laboratories
And textbooks about tolerating diversity.

But the old man only had high-deductible health insurance
That paid for nothing.
Healers had always prayed to *him* . . .
To deliver fresh white blankets of respite to hillsides exhausted by
endless growth.

His strength was the throwing of fresh, soft snowfalls
At children in need of fireside arms to comfort them
With long lessons about history
And how to twist fibers into survival and memories.

For the next three hundred years,
North Wind stumbled about with his head down,
In and out among jack pines and summer cottages
On the peripheries of each of the watersheds,

With nickels jangling in his pockets like muffled wind chimes.

He wanted to sleep
Or to pass on his responsibilities,
But he had made a commitment
To deliver his services predictably and infinitely.

He swam through dense water's edge balsams,
Parting northern airs in a rippling breaststroke,
At each Anishinaabe village slipping into a kitchen chair
By the cookstoves of knowledge keepers and clan elders,

Instructing each to lean forward, double over,
Soft, giving, and invisible
Until limited opportunities flowed from their lungs to the tops of tall
spruce trees;
But he inadvertently spread the virus like kindness.

The old men used to have a fish camp
On the north shore of Lake Superior,
Where they rested in doldrums between rainstorms
And stockpiled birch logs and fragrant balsam.

Summers, South Wind would join them,
The three playing three-handed pinochle,
Shuffling and dealing out barometric pressures,
Waiting for the Anishinaabeg to finish harvesting wild blueberries and
rice . . .

So that they could play doubles with pairs
Teamed up against one another,
Opposing forces and neediness battling for matchsticks
With childish smiles on their faces.

The three old men would strip down to their long johns,

Shuffling and bidding on the next season's windstorms.
They left the kitchen table long enough
To scatter fish eggs and pollen
While they chewed on long strips of dry, smoked lake trout.

South Wind stopped coming after de Soto came up the Mississippi
Spreading measles and smallpox
To unsuspecting villages
Where his soldiers had been greeted with smiles and fresh oysters.

It was all South Wind could do to cope with the decomposing bodies.
He wanted to cover each of his relatives' eyes and ears
With clamshells and love songs,
To bury them under undulating earth mounds
In the shapes of snaking rivers.

But after three weeks, he began burning the bodies,
Piled all together with woven dreams and social norms,
Up and down the sine-generated curves and oxbows
Of the river that went on forever.

Eventually even this was insufficient,
And the old man covered over village after village
With great hurricanes of silt and suffocating mud,
With songbirds for grave goods,
Snapped twigs as utensils in their afterlives.

Now the old men never saw South Wind, except in anger,
Barging through forest-cleared cornfields and parking lots,
Spitting at green John Deere combines
And historic barns preserved on broad, treeless homesteads,

Mumbling incomprehensible curses about livestock and spawning grounds,
Flailing with both hands open wide,
Trying to trap remnant individuals of extinct species of snails

Between his stiff, bent fingers.

West Wind and North Wind push against their work boots,
Adjust their backs against dry, crumbling sandbanks,
Comfortable in the curve of the narrow ravine,
Smelling of too-thick coffee and dust from old bones.

West Wind holds his breath,
Pours steaming coffee into a pair of dark clay bowls.
The old men sip and blink, shuffle and deal,
Every third reach spilling three cold playing cards . . .

Into the empty grit space of the unpredictable dummy hand.
They miss their old friend.
He had helped them remember the values of the various meld
So that they knew how to bid
On the next season's growth spurts and thunderstorms.

West Wind fingers his share of the well-worn deck.
He shifts his stiff knees, spills out his cold coffee, and suddenly
breaks wind.
North Wind coughs phlegm into a soft handkerchief made of smoke-
tanned muskrat,
Complains about the sulfuric, polluting stench.

West Wind blames an upwind iron smelter from across the Canadian
border.
"There is no upwind. You *are* the wind, you old fool."
They chuckle like only old companions can chuckle,
Trapped in a narrow ravine with their obligations and longing,
Where sunlight goes lost in walls of depth.

Groaning and tired, each reaches to uncurl a snail of coiled downy
feathers.
West Wind stands to urinate onto the hardwood coals.

The two old winds stretch their bones against their confines and clear
their lungs,
Each tossing his share of the old deck toward the approaching
darkness.

Those smooth, soft playing cards fly over subdivisions and shopping
malls,
Over the heads of prairie chickens and coyotes,
Dip into dry ravines and scrape against sandbanks.
They blow along I-94, where the highway crosses the river that goes
on forever.

Two lanes from a collapsed bridge have been pulled together
On fragile struts of iron, silver dollars, and concrete,
Where the jack of diamonds and queen of spades skitter over the
guardrail . . .
And glide down the Mississippi,
Past shipping canals and levees, all the way to the Gulf of Mexico.

Somewhere along a strand west of the Apalachicola River
Upwind from the rhythmic thrum of a seaside condominium resort,
East Wind pauses on his haunches under moonlight
Between hurricanes and family obligations

. . . To run his fingers through white sands
And sift pink surf clams from green ones.
In idleness,
He waits for his brothers to deal him in,
So he can bet on his meld of moisture and heat.

The jack of diamonds is still smooth and cool to the touch,
Like a sheet of ice.
It is comforting,
Like the lips of a loving woman . . .

And for no other reason than his own satisfaction,
East Wind walks for lifetimes
Across Louisiana and Texas, in sinuous loops around blooming
hillsides and swales,
From green to red,
From moisture to desiccation.

At each town and farmstead
He sings wagering songs
And plays barefoot kickball
With screeching children and laughing old men.

Somewhere before an invisible border with Mexico,
East Wind gives the smooth jack a quick, cold flick
Toward a Sonoran hillside,
Where it lodges in the rigid branches of a scrub oak
And smiles in silence through unblinking eyes.

. . . So the old man gives a final sigh
Before turning his arthritic frame back toward the gulf.
The old jack reaches for that last gasp of moist air,
Tumbles across a rocky streambed, and comes to tenuous rest
In a narrow valley's fence line of demanding river willows and fragrant
cedars.

This makes the Kickapoo very happy,
For the jack of diamonds has been missing from their deck
For a long, long time.
The queen of spades has been replaced with a joker
Who will remain among them for several generations.

HURRICANE KATRINA

They are sitting in a warm September, those Indians
Leaning back on their palms, legs stretched out in front of them.
Tired, already put in more hours than most people by 11:00 a.m.
Already put in a full eight hours by the time most folks finish lunch.

They are sitting in a warm September, those Indians
Finding shelter, comfort, shade, solace, next to the bumper of an old,
familiar work truck.
Old-familiar-truck-bumper like a magnet for Indians,
Like fishing bait, you wanna catch Indians . . .

They are sitting in a warm September, those Indians
In the shady part of the yard,
Dogs on chains, can't let 'em run loose, bother those folks living on
most of the allotment, used to be ours.
Kids in house doing curriculum homework from the tribe, can't let
them go to public schools, not safe.

They are sitting in a warm September, those Indians
Fingers running over smooth cucumbers, too big, too many,
Fingers running over smooth summer squash, too big, too many.
That's OK, Indians eat them, like words in a textbook.

They are sitting in a warm September, those Indians
Every shade of brown. Green half-breed eyes, big, like raccoon-
knows-it's-gonna-be-dinner eyes.
Long, wide, pretty-man full-blood eyes.
Wide, almond, three-quarter-blood eyes.
Round and searching forgotten-in-the-legal-definitions eyes.

They are sitting in a warm September, those Indians
Shoulda picked sweetgrass, got too busy.

The pow wow sellers got to it before us. Basket-makin' ain't worth the time no more.
People desperate, sellin' the sacred-plant-of-the-north, sure sign of BAD TIMES.

They are sitting in a warm September, those Indians
Leaning forward off of those palms, talking quiet and close.
Been readin' the news, listenin' to the radio,
Readin' between the lines, about the genocide.

They are sitting in a warm September, those Indians
Readin' about how they could have done those levies different down in New Orleans,
Where they drowned all those people on purpose,
Black people, brown people, unemployed people, hospital people, handicapped people.
(Saved the real estate, though.)

They are sitting in a warm September, those Indians
Thinking about it, but so painful nobody talks about it,
That epidemic killed all those Indians; lucky it wasn't us.
Killed our grandmothers. Killed our grandfathers. Killed our aunties, our uncles, our mothers' older sisters, older brothers; hell, even the dogs died, nobody to take care of them.

They are sitting in a warm September, those Indians
Thinking about it, but so painful nobody talks about it,
That state highway closed off during that epidemic, no doctors let in, no medicines let in.
Just fear let in.
They say, *We know what genocide looks like.*

They are sitting in a warm September, those Indians
Knowing about the decaying bodies that survivors are getting sick from, forced to deal with them all alone,
Knowing about the lack of food and water and shelter,

Knowing about the lack of opportunities and the lack of jobs used to justify letting nature
Kill the "weak and useless,"
Outlined in a Charles Darwin textbook about banking and finance.

They are sitting in a warm September, those Indians
Thinking, *They thought they could get away with it,*
Thinking, *The nerve of those land and resource usurpers,*
Thinking, *Good Americans won't let them get away with it.*

They are sitting in a warm September, those Indians
Great Lakes are so warm, fish are unpredictable
Just now, when we finally got our fishing rights back.
Indians can't get enough fish to survive on, sure sign of BAD TIMES.

They are sitting in a warm September, those Indians
People tellin' 'em, go north, go south, go urban, so we can have your real estate;
Go north, go south, go urban, so we can have your jobs, your farming, your hunting;
Go north, go south, go urban, so we can have your fish, your treaty rights, your history,
Your *stories.*

They are sitting in a warm September, those Indians
Talking in hushed tones, so their children don't hear
Talking in hushed tones, so predators cannot hear
Their residual fear.
We know what genocide looks like.

HARVEST ME

Harvest me.

I've been waiting on this light tree branch, too small and invisible to inconvenience even the slightest breeze,

So protective of the brightest bits of my plumage in hopes that you would discover and desire at first only the dullest, earth-toned parts of me

So that we could come together in survival and a long-term relationship that would ensure that even I would survive

Your crossing of oceans to find me, even if by mistake, naming me after distant continents and your own preconceptions.

Harvest me.

I've been tumbling about between volcanic heavings and subduction zones, under mats woven of old oceanic concretions and temper tantrums,

Children crying searing lava that hardened on my breast and froze my arms into permanent embraces

Until waves and currents of heavy water and thin air wore through the rhyolite fabric and bared my skin

Along that seam on my breastbone where the feathers part and soft warmth seeps out to nurture nuzzling, hungry chicks.

Harvest me.

I've felt my blood vessels swell, leaching nutrients outward to every dendritic outcropping,

Filling each stress-induced crevice and overused internal organ with silicate agate scar tissues and metallic inclusions,

Filling heavy skull bones with porous mineral tenacity and lobes of neck tissue with fluid-filled bulging musculature

So that I can plant my feet in valleys and stand strong while you slam against me in your perceived reproductive war over resources that were never meant to be hoarded.

Harvest me.

I've been heaved onto buckboards, shoveled into sluices, ground up, pelletized, and shipped down canals and rivers

To upwind smelters belching acidic rains that dissolve my algae and float my elvers and minnows upward

To poison my songbirds and rip the cries of gulls from the undulation of my coastlines' soft breasts,

As though this could emulate the life-giving ashes that settle from east to west, creating time zones of respite from Mount Saint Helens to Vesuvius.

Harvest me.

I've been celebrating gravity in this deep canyon for hundreds of thousands of sandstorms, riding horseback on mists and cloudlines across dry skyways,

Grabbing handfuls of prevailing winds, always looking below me, for greedy mountaintops to snatch at the heaviest accumulations of fat around my belly

Stored temporarily in my tissues, for use by later generations even farther downhill,

Where pine roots and cactus-dwelling lizards stretch under woven patterns of songblankets worn by the moisture clan, the sandstone clan, the tomorrow clan,

And we dig deep wells into aquifers of lifeblood with our feet as we pound out our seasonal ceremonies, using fossils as rattles and our tail feathers as drums.

Harvest me.

I've been swimming without eyes in the motionless pools of an underground fortress, subsisting on guano-fed larvae

In the hopes that when you discovered me, you would see beauty in my transparent tissues and obvious bulging blood vessels,

Heart-pumped diesel bloodlines in an odorless, colorless, damp space punctuated by the *drip, drip, drip* of saturated hopes,

The experiences of my children tied up in small bundles of calico-wrapped preservation, stored-up knowledge and traditional rainstorms

Disguised as store-bought tobacco, shrink-wrapped in refined placental tissues and labeled with recycled old growth from the hairlines of tribal elders.

Harvest me.

I've been teaching my children to wait out snowstorms under heavy-bent boughs of paint-thick knowledge,

Where grouse puff up neck feathers and slow down their breathing in anticipation of inspiring impudent tattoos during inconsistent spring thaws,

Cultural downpours of satellite transmissions and tornadoes of microwave radiowaves howling with mace and rubber bullets,

Public school–induced statistical pellets and low expectations broadcast like pollen to engineer failure and plummeting,

While children press ears against my breast and listen to experience sung by persistent currents and the droning crush of bones in slow-moving jaws.

Harvest me.

I've been waiting on this prairie, huddling with extinct horses for warmth, with decomposing grasses on our cumulative breath,

Preserving moisture and bacteria that pack themselves under my bark and glow during silence to attract mates and hitch a ride to the next pow wow,

Where they will disguise themselves as bright feathers and polishable gemstones to distract recent arrivals

From places where my salt sings love songs to those who need its electrical bonding and financial buoyancy.

Harvest me.

I've been wrapped in soft hand-tanned doeskin and waterproof birch bark painted with ochre's historical instructions,

And warriors transported me under their basswood fiber shirts against the coals of their breasts, running across deserts, under cliffs, over streambeds and interstate highways,

Handing me off one by one, to strength and competence, age and youth, long reaching fingers grasping at the preservation of my accumulations

Buried under dry gravel in inland-facing upper caves, reached only by wooden scaffolds later burned by my ancestors.

Harvest me.

I've been waiting on this light tree branch, too small and invisible to inconvenience even the slightest breeze,

So protective of the brightest bits of my plumage in hopes that you would discover and desire at first only the dullest, earth-toned parts of me

So that we could come together in survival and a long-term relationship that would ensure that even I would survive

Your crossing of oceans to find me, even if by mistake, naming me after distant continents and your own preconceptions.

Harvest me.

FICTION VERSUS NONFICTION

I've noticed
that at the Library of Congress
they have a hard time with the concept of nonfiction and fiction
merging,
as though it could be any different.
So librarians
dutifully tuck "history books" into the realm of nonfiction,
as they have been so carefully taught,

preserving
the myths of our culture,
the ones we have learned all our lives.
At universities.
At public schools.
In day care.
In front of the TV.
At the kitchen table.
In our mothers' bellies.

Myths
about dominance and superiority
and who owns what and who owns whom.
Dignity. Respect. Good jobs.
Continents.

on Oral Histories about President Number Sixteen

He's on American currency. On American dollars. On American coins. On American stamps. America gave him an annual holiday. He's an American hero, it's said.

America has an entire oral history about him. He did things heroes are supposed to have done. He had his flaws. But he was a good guy. Exemplified all that is good about America. The America of which he is a chapter. A chapter constantly renewed and summed up for present-day desires for America

to paint

herself.

He's on America's currency. On America's dollars. On America's coins. On America's stamps. America gave him an annual holiday. He's an American hero, it's said.

We have heroes, too. They are on our cultural currency.

Not on dollars. On our expectations of acceptable behavior regarding distribution of resources.

Not on coins. On our commitment to protect and nurture our children and others who are vulnerable.

Not on stamps. On our intent to forgive youth and ignorance and move toward maintenance of cultural health, healing of nicks and wounds. Fingertips burnt. Noses pinched. Entire cultures maimed. Discredited. (Every day is their holiday.)

They are not on our dollars. Not on our coins. Not on our stamps. No annual holiday. Our equivalents to those things were systematically attacked. Replaced with "costumes." With emblems. With quaint history books. Monocultural patriotic chants. Primitive. Childish. Witch-craft. Speaking in tongues. Political shamans. Royalty. Princesses. Chiefs. Commanders in chief. Icons imposed upon us. With currency.

  With coins.

                With stamps.

                        With annual holidays.

America's heroes should be our heroes, too, we are told.

  No.

        Thank.

                You.

America's hero freed the slaves, it is said.

But he hung the Indians, we whisper.

He's your hero. We do not believe.

(The occasional historian announces that he was a good guy after all because he reviewed the trial transcripts one by one and only hung some of them—the boys, too.)

(But he never hung a Confederate for leading a revolt.)

He's on America's currency. All those dead Indians.

  On America's dollars. Hung, together.

  On America's coins. Holding hands, singing, praying.

  On America's stamps. Until their legs kicked and stilled. *He has an annual holiday.* It happened over there, on the other side of the lake. *He's America's hero,* it is said.

Number Sixteen has an annual holiday.

Poor America: she cannot transfer her checks into currency on that day. Postage stamps are useless on that day.

We can protect and nurture our children on that day. Forgive youth and ignorance. Fingertips burnt. Noses pinched. Legs and feet of men and boys dangling, twitching, grabbing for solid ground that America's hero reached out and snatched from under them. (While their mothers watched!) Entire cultures discredited. Books and educational curriculum guides renamed as "scrolls," "pictographs," "legends."

Our heroes are our histories. On our cultural equivalent of currencies. Not on dollars. (They learned by their mistakes.) Not on coins. (Their foibles.) Not on stamps. (Their weaknesses.) Every day is their holiday. (Their strengths.)

I have the honor to inform you that the thirty-eight Indians and half-breeds, ordered by you for execution, were hung yesterday at Mankato, at 10:00 a.m.

SHHH . . .

Shhh . . .
Now here's a secret . . .
Do they know?
That at the turn of this 21st century, in this state . . .
That the ethnic group with the highest number of college diplomas was
Native American women,
And that the ethnic group with the highest unemployment was
Native American women
Followed by Native American men.

Shhh . . .
I promise not to talk about this . . .
As long as they let me clean house for them
At an acceptable wage for my credentials and mindset,
For just a few hours or even all day until dark,
After they celebrate Thanksgiving with their loved ones
And they leave me some sliced turkey
In the refrigerator
Next to the block of molding cheese
Behind the sour milk
And a slice of fiber-less bread with a bite taken out of it.

Shhh . . .
I won't complain . . .
As long as they come visit me
At the neighborhood craft fair
Where they've included a caricature of me in demonstration of their inclusiveness
And color blindness to our lack of futures and 99 percent off-reservation unemployment
That we carefully mask with imported seed beads

Woven into trinkets
To hang about the necks of children and grandchildren
To remind them that their entitlement includes giving themselves
Indian names,
Like *Fuzzy Nobody Bear* and *Little Two Feet Dancing for Nothing,*
Maybe even come up with a good one for the dog.

Shhh . . .
Now here's a secret . . .
Do they know?
That we've been giving ourselves Indian names . . .
Since before the turn of this 21st century, in this state . . .
Since before they invented the concept of base-10 centuries
Built upon the supposed births of saviors and entitlers . . .
Since before they decided to mine resources on a scale larger
Than anything they thought we could perceive,
We gave ourselves Indian names . . .
Names like:

     Woman Who Crushes Rocks Between Her
      Teeth
    Man Who Stands at a Precipice with Anger
Protector of Clans and Futures
       Law School Graduate
   Doctor
    Mother

        Father

   Loving Son
Hardworking Daughter
     Equal
   Nemesis
Deed-Holder to Future Mineral Rights
    Protector of Amphibians Out of Range of Vision
     Tomorrow
   Today
Always.

Shhh . . .
Guess . . .
Guess which state.
Guess what date.
Guess when fluid borders were set in india ink on their maps to their futures.
Guess when dots and dashes guaranteed dominance
And purchased intent to pretend
That making chattel slavery illegal
And closing boarding schools
And letting poor people buy lottery tickets
Put an end to slavery,
Stopped killing Indian children,
And made equal opportunity available to everyone.

Nimiigwechwiaag Nigitiziimag

I Thank Them (for sending me to university)

After I gave up on the strength of my parents
to push back against their Indian status,
and I forgot about warm waters and safe cliffs
and bellies full of mild fresh fish, turtles, crayfish, clams, and tender
frogs' legs,

And I had discovered the possibilities of education
if only I would leave behind the calm and comfort of their sacrifices,
I would wake up late at night and remember to thank them
by swimming across the shipping canal from Houghton to Hancock
accompanied by small brown mathematical moles
as though it were something any coed could do
whether the moonlight was there or not
strengthening my muscles
so that I could show them back home
that I had learned lessons from them about strength.

Back home, I would swim from one island to another
across currents that kept moose calves safe from hungry wolves
and worried my parents
who had grown old
from keeping me safe
and were aware of their weakness,
even as I swam away from their grasp
beyond the reach of their strong arms and common sense and
lifetimes of experience
in deceptively warm waters
that turn deadly cold with the whims of winds bigger than mere
Indians.

Listen to Your Mother

I know who you are, because I saw you one day, dancing on my grave
As though I were already deceased, and you had title to my happiness.

I know who you are, because I heard you one day, challenging my credentials
As though I didn't earn my PhD in earth science by shrinking and swelling.

I remember the song that you and your friends sang about entitlement
And your rights to use my flesh as raw materials for short-term commitments.

I listened with my ear close to the surface while you bragged loudly about plans
To shake me until my blood vessels broke and my heart pumped oil to the surface.

I remember how you foolishly thought that rich fats and oils ran through my body
Instead of sweet water comprising the bulk of my blood and tissues.

I remember your laughter when you thought you could record my heartbeats
As sheet music for pop stars to thrust through the airwaves I wore like a skin.

I sent my breezes from west to east like seismic attitude sensors
To feel if you were paying attention to my chest-pounding screams and scolding.

I know who you are, because I taught you to speak, before you learned to shriek

About the joys of one-night stands with internal combustion engines.

I remember the way you grabbed at bits of sunshine like jewels in a
night sky,
Certain that my sweat and precipitation would never limit your
visibility.

I know who you are, because I taught you to walk over my own giving
bones
Before you learned to sneak out at night for intoxicating cocktails of
misconception.

I know who you are, because I recognized the adolescent tilt in your
voice
When you insisted that you knew more than I did about my own cash
value.

I know who you are, because I continued to feed you when you
returned home
From long nights of partying on my precipices with your
inexperienced cohorts.

I remember the day I taught you to swim in thick waters rippling with
invertebrates
Before you brought home your high school diploma in advanced
socioeconomic advantage.

I know who you are, because I felt you probing for my house key
Under the porch light I turned on every twenty-eight days hoping you
would find your way home.

I remember the smell of your urine as you passed on contaminants
through culverts
Intended to strangle the weak and bypass generational responsibility.

I know who you are, because I watched pounding waves of saltwater and air
Bounce back from the refined oil–black business suit you wore to my funeral.

I know who you are, because I saw you one day, dancing on my grave
As though I were already deceased, and you had title to my biomass.

I know who you are, because I have fingers stretched out to the four directions,
To the heavens and to the depths beyond bedrock, where I am hot and fluid.

I know who you are, because I feel the coming and going of your footfalls,
Whether soft and wanting, angry and demanding, or dissipating and alone.

I know who you are, because I have felt you crawl across the wrinkles of my skin
Eagerly seeking bits of decomposing rock and biology to nibble away at for only one small lifetime.

Above Me, Below Me

Thrown away, every which way, with no regard to the Four Directions
Or the importance of Above and Below and their sacrosanct status
To the thousands of ancestors who came before him, preserving culture,
Mountains and soil, biodiversity, history, demographics, and the delicate balance
Between plants and bedrock, the weight of water and the wispiness of air,
The density of predation and the airiness of souls, the need to devour and the need to birthe . . .

The boy lived in bits and pieces in textureless voids between usurpation and denigration,
Inconveniencing the benefactors of his prey-like status with his fawn-like squeals
For safety in invisibility and minimal expectations for energy expended
By the thousands of ancestors who came before him, his mother's hawk-like screams for sensibility and sharing
Unheeded by the superordinate outsiders' dominance of Institutional Control
Over the Four Directions, completely ignoring Above and Below and their sacrosanct status.

It is said that the child was gifted to his people by those Four Directions,
His mother a docile eastern zephyr, impregnated from Above and Below,
Nursed and educated in childbearing by strong sister winds from the west,
While mothers and aunties from the north kept her hydrated and well-rested,

Southern grandmothers gathered and dried medicines to be steeped for strong blood teas,
And bedrock lay patiently in wait, storing heat and prayers for a quick and safe delivery . . .

Of hopes and expectations for moist survival among cracks in dried earth,
On hard lava shores beaten by ghost winds and ever-present time,
In the stalks of heat-seared grasses and the mandibles of enthusiastic adolescent insects,
Between the stars of night sky's stealth of sunshine's patient radiance,
Between the milky texture of mist and the electric dryness of lightning's long, demanding reach,
And the embracing nature of human hope and bone-crushing education by errors and flaws.

This boy sang to the Four Directions and the essential presence of Above and Below,
Composed Clan Songs, overtures, and contemporary rock operas with his first rhythmic breaths
While great lakes and wide rivers improvised percussive accompaniments,
Waves pounding, demanding attention and nutrients, then inserting rests,
Long empty spaces that demanded we tilt our heads, hold our breath, and listen with our hearts
Until bellowing elk bulls provided long, low backdrops to the chirping of small green branches rubbing against one another . . .

Echoes resounding between cliff faces and soft mosses on rift-made ledges
Where iron and copper and silicates seeped through for millions of years
In anticipation of the child's need for sharp blades, fishhooks, and cooking stones

To soften the hard bodies of tall trees and fish, to crack open long bones
Full of soft marrow and succulence, stored ions and sunshine, careful futures and harsh demands,
For coping mechanisms and transformations among changing environments and unpredictability.

Unpredictability became his swaddling, while the Four Directions twisted their arms around the boy,
Wrapped him in snowstorms, interwoven with ragged sleet and hail, intended to shield him
And to strengthen his skin with periodic abrasion in small packets of respite and scar tissue
So that he could fight inevitable battles with outside elements oblivious to the importance of Above and Below and the desperate wind-calls of the Four Directions
That birthed him, caressed him, and eventually released their sinuous grasp on their geologic hopes,
And let him slide away from their tissues into empty spaces where predation filtered in like dissolved minerals.

This boy sauntered out from tall canyons' doorstep with iron and wild mint teas on his breath,
His pockets laden with life lessons on how to write down his history with red and yellow ochres,
How to translate chemical formulas backward and forward with nut-dyed porcupine quills,
How to measure mathematical moles with smooth trade beads and hailstones,
How to compose seasonal concerts from kernels of corn snow and wild rice
While reading out loud from the ancient molecular patterns of constellations and auroras

As predatory masters and mistresses remained in wait, well-fed attitudes coiled

To perceive any threatening effort at competence and success
In the thin, unsupportive, dry air of empty spaces they had crafted
from their own affluence
For the unsuspecting children of the Four Directions and their wind-
borne presence as testimony
To the sacrosanct nature of Above and Below to the generations that
came before this boy,
Creating a matrix void of buoyancy for the flailing limbs and soft,
surprised cries of the vulnerable child.

The boy practiced new histories and threw his ochre crayons into
distant ravines,
Tore at the skin and birch bark foundations of glistening quilled
chemical equations,
Tossed corn snow and hailstones every which way, with no regard to
the Four Directions,
While he traveled through dark snowstorms to mandatory school
concerts,
Where he transformed his Clan Songs into Christmas carols and sang
the desperate translations ever louder,
Begging for praise and survival, while taunts and accusations swam
thick between molecules of oxygen and loon feathers.

This boy's hawk-mother cried out from between boulders and
volcanic rifts,
The winds of the Four Directions rushed in to resuscitate him with
oxygen-rich traditions and songs,
Laid ancestors and histories of competence, survival, and longevity in
his path,
Each subsequently crushed by diesel-black wheels of slow-moving
Institutional invasive species
And loud, hot shrieks of arrogance, self-proclaimed supremacy, and
access to resources
That blasted carbon monoxide–blistered hope into roadside ditches
of lead contamination and minnow-choking weedbeds.

Loose sands twirled every which way, with no regard to the Four
Directions
Or the importance of Above and Below and their sacrosanct status
To the thousands of ancestors who came before him, preserving
culture,
Mountains and soil, biodiversity, history, demographics, and the
delicate balance
Between plants and bedrock, the weight of water and the wispiness of
air,
The density of predation and the airiness of souls, the need to devour
and the need to birthe . . .

The boy dissolved into bits and pieces in textureless voids between
usurpation and denigration,
For inconveniencing the benefactors of his prey-like status with his
fawn-like squeals
For safety in invisibility and minimal expectations for energy
expended
By the thousands of ancestors who came before him, his mother's
hawk-like screams for sensibility and sharing
Unheeded by the superordinate outsiders' dominance of Institutional
Control
Over the Four Directions, completely ignoring Above and Below and
their sacrosanct status.

It is said that the child was gifted to his people by those Four
Directions,
His mother a docile eastern zephyr, impregnated from Above and
Below,
Nursed and educated in childbearing by strong sister winds from the
west,
While mothers and aunties from the north kept her hydrated and well-
rested,
Southern grandmothers gathered and dried medicines to be steeped
for strong blood teas,

And bedrock lay patiently in wait, storing heat and prayers for a quick and safe delivery . . .

Of hopes and expectations for socioeconomic equality and access to employment and opportunities,
With careful regard to the Four Directions and the importance of Above and Below and their sacrosanct status
To the thousands of ancestors who came before him and the thousands who will come after him,
Standing among rocks and in mucous-thick muds, in the density of challenge and the airiness of hope,
With arms outstretched to grasp at inclusiveness and belonging, moving
In a matrix of praise and prose, music and errors, glacier-tumbled rocks and calcium-rich accomplishments . . .

Let this boy saunter out from tall canyons' doorsteps with minerals and wild teas on his breath,
His pockets laden with life lessons on how to write down history with red and yellow ochres,
How to translate chemical formulas backward and forward with shining porcupine quills,
How to measure mathematical moles with smooth trade beads and hailstones,
How to compose volumes and arias from kernels of corn snow and wild rice,
While singing out loud from the ancient molecular patterns of constellations, geology, and auroras . . .

That were gifted to him by the Four Directions and from Above and Below with careful regard to his sacrosanct status.

On Mountains

On the mainland,
Every once in a while,
A Lake Superior Ojibwe opens up his fists,
Lets go of Lake Superior,
To grasp at loose rocks
Bearing promises of mainstream footfalls.

This is where he is when he is not there.
This is where he makes currency out of pebbles.
This is a place he takes advantage of,
Or it takes advantage of him.
This place sings songs about apartheid.

Mainland mountains sing him confused songs about erosion.
Where hills are gentle and glacial-hewn,
The open spaces benign and green.
The sun claims to find soil and living spaces between small trees,
Without mountains of lava or granite.

The mountains are human-hewn.
They are mountains of separation,
Where history and clan songs struggle
To find soil and living spaces,
Blocked from carnal knowledge of one another
By sands harsh, infertile, and slick,
Mountainsides fashioned from concrete, reinforced with attitude.

On the mainland,
Every once in a while,
A Lake Superior Ojibwe opens up his fists,
Lets go of Lake Superior,
To slide down the coast into a city,

For just long enough to lose confidence
In himself and his grannies.

Old expectations,
Old coastlines full of broken paddles
Old ducks swimming in dark circles under old stories about old men;
It can make your daddy look like nobody
Under a cloud of moonless nights,
Where no one sings the power of wind or waves
Or ice that will cut through your wrist like a knife.

On the open water,
Every once in a while,
A Lake Superior Ojibwe opens up his fists,
Grabs at moisture-laden skies,
And sings long, loud songs
In shouting matches with gulls and thunderbirds.

BAWAATING

I don't understand
Why the Jesuits and their descendants
Named the outlet of Lake Superior the Saint Mary's River
After the mother of their god,

When generations told us
That a wild and youthful ancestor
Broke down the giant beaver dam
That held in millions of snowmelts.

He was bickering with a relative,
Setting a perfect example of how not to behave,
When he unleashed the rapids
And split our world in two,

Forcing us to learn new skills,
Like standing up in short canoes
To reach down with long spears
For sustenance.

It is because of this huge lake
And its big rushing rivers
That we grew long leg bones
And were labeled as giants.

I don't understand
Why the makers of modern maps
Named a rock in the water
The Devil's Chair,

When generations told us
That a wild and youthful ancestor
Is resting in that spot after jumping
West to East across the big lake.

He was showing off for his brothers,
Setting a perfect example of how not to behave,
When he jumped and nobody saw it,
So he has to do it over and over,

Until we all stop by in our vessels
To tell him we saw him,
And that we are proud of his strength and resilience,
As he sits there and whispers back how much he loves us.

I don't understand
Why the Jesuits and their descendants
Named the water swirling around those rocks
The Devil's Frying Pans,

When my uncle ran his boat onto those rocks
After the wind went to sleep
And the white swirls subsided,
So he sits there now and waves a tall spruce tree.

We know he is there to steer us away
From boat-crushing reefs
And wind-driven currents
That shift with the whims of wild and youthful ancestors and their life
stories.

Dark Days, Long Nights

A Conversation Between Women Writers of Color

(Just a Cautious Conversation)

Brown Woman A: I am worried about our safety.
Brown Woman B: I am worried about our literature.
Brown Woman C: Our literature is a thin film that wraps itself around us and protects us from outside incursions into our ability to procreate.

Brown Woman A: I am worried about our literature.
Brown Woman B: I am worried about our place on this continent.

Brown Woman A: I am worried about our place on this continent.
Brown Woman C: I am worried that we look to other continents for a homeland.

Brown Woman A: I am worried that we look to other continents for a homeland.
Brown Woman C: I am worried that our homeland doesn't make us comfortable.

Brown Woman A: I am worried that our homeland doesn't make us comfortable.
Brown Woman B: I am worried that successful Black literature must look to Africa for satisfaction.

Brown Woman A: I am worried that successful Black literature must look to Africa for satisfaction.
Brown Woman C: I am worried that successful Native American literature must look to South America for validation.

Brown Woman A: I am worried that successful Native American literature must look to South America for validation.
Brown Woman C: I am worried that we look elsewhere because America doesn't give us a home.

Brown Woman A: I am worried that we look elsewhere because America doesn't give us a home.
Brown Woman B: I am worried that we don't feel welcome here.

Brown Woman A: I am worried that we don't feel welcome here.
Brown Woman C: Are they worried that *WE* is so strong?

Brown Woman A: Are they worried that *WE* is so strong?
Brown Woman B: I am worried that brown, dark, different, *OTHER* is so strong . . .

Brown Woman A: I am worried that brown, dark, different, *OTHER* is so strong . . .
Brown Woman C: I am worried that *DIFFERENT* is so strong . . .

Brown Woman A: I am worried that *DIFFERENT* is so strong . . .
Brown Woman B: I am worried that the elite's grasping at status quo is so strong . . .
Brown Woman C: Does rejection send our ambition far away to look to different continents for acceptance?

Brown Woman A: I am worried that the fragility of our place in the universe keeps us afraid.
Brown Woman C: I am worried that we look to Africa, Europe, South America . . .

Brown Woman A: I am worried that we look to Africa, Europe, South America . . .
Brown Woman B: I am worried that we look to *OTHER* places and people for desperate fantasies about survival.

Brown Woman A: I am worried that we look to *OTHER* places and people for desperate fantasies about survival.
Brown Woman C: I am worried that we do not feel at home here.

Brown Woman A: I am worried that we do not feel at home here.
Brown Woman B: We are denied competence, safety, and a place to call *HOME* here.

Brown Woman A: We are denied competence, safety, and a place to call *HOME* here.
Brown Woman C: I am worried that we have no choice but to fantasize about feeling at home somewhere else.
Brown Woman A: I am worried that we will always fantasize about feeling at home somewhere else.
Brown Woman B: I am worried that we've been trapped in our own modern literature, writing about elsewhere as home.

Brown Woman A: I am worried that we've been trapped in our own modern literature, writing about elsewhere as home.
Brown Woman C: I am worried that we've been trapped in our own modern literature, writing about *ANOTHER TIME* as home.

Brown Woman A: I am worried that here is not home for us all.
Brown Woman B: I am worried that we seek solace outside of this place and time.

Brown Woman A: I am worried that we seek solace outside of this place and time.
Brown Woman C: I am worried that we might be acceptable here and now only as cleaners of toilets.

Brown Woman A: I am worried that we might be acceptable here and now only as cleaners of toilets.
Brown Woman B: I am worried that we are acceptable only as receptacles of donations others choose to share.

Brown Woman C: I am worried that we are tossed too little to engender self-respect.

Brown Woman A: I am worried that we are tossed too little to engender self-respect.
Brown Woman B: I am worried for too few survival hours, too little acceptance of our labor and our gifts . . .

Brown Woman A: I am worried for too few survival hours, too little acceptance of our labor and our gifts . . .
Brown Woman C: I am worried by my fear of fighting the status quo in favor of survival.

Brown Woman A: I am worried by *MY* fear of fighting the status quo in favor of survival.
Brown Woman B: I am worried for settling for less than full first-class citizenship.

Brown Woman A: I am worried that *BROWN* is so strong . . .
Brown Woman B: I am worried that we frighten the majority, the superordinate.
Brown Woman C: What words are acceptable for describing this? I feel like a textbook.

Brown Woman A: I am worried that we frighten the majority, the superordinate.
Brown Woman B: I am worried that *YOU* are so strong . . .

Brown Woman A: I am worried that *YOU* are so strong . . .
Brown Woman C: I am worried that your voice shakes the universe.

Brown Woman A: I am worried that **YOUR** voice shakes the universe.
Brown Woman C: I am worried that threats of death and termination of future generations keep us from shaking too hard.

Brown Woman A: I am worried that threats of death and termination of future generations keep us from shaking too hard.
Brown Woman B: I am afraid that you won't shake; please shake.

Brown Woman A: I am afraid that you won't shake.
Brown Woman B: Please shake with me.
Brown Woman C: I am still worried that threats of death and termination of future generations keep us from shaking too hard.

Brown Woman A: I am worried that threats of death and termination of future generations keep us from shaking too hard.
Brown Woman B: I am worried that the fragility of our place in the universe keeps us afraid.
Brown Woman C: I am giving you permission to sing, shout, thrash your arms, and wail.

Brown Woman A: I am giving you permission to be a powerful woman.
Brown Woman B: I am giving you permission to be a Toad Woman, a Thundercloud Woman, a Shaking the Earth Woman . . .

Brown Woman A: I am giving you permission to plant roots in the earth where you stand.
Brown Woman B: I am giving you permission to reach up to the sky and grab fistfuls of access and success.
Brown Woman C: I am giving you permission to swing your intellect about you freely, like a child spinning with outstretched arms.

Brown Woman A: I am giving you permission to pray out loud.
Brown Woman B: I am giving you permission to stomp your feet!
Brown Woman C: I am giving you permission to grasp your future with iron fists that are welded to your tomorrows with determination, hope, and possibilities.

ANISHINAABE WOMEN

Sisters of these great lakes unfold themselves
Ancient waves swelling with the silt of uncountable generations
They have wrestled with underwater panthers and bears
Great sturgeons and giant antlered snakes

They thrust upwards against
Manifest destiny and the doctrine of discovery
Immense rolling thunderstorms
With fangs of lightning and cleansing fire

Sisters of these great lakes kick to the surface
Pushing against the sandy bottoms and rocky escarpments
Of their own waterborne depths
One with waves of manifest history and belonging

Sisters of these great lakes extend themselves beyond their horizons
Swelling with the heat of uncountable generations
Bypassing underwater panthers and bears
Great sturgeons and giant antlered snakes

They waft over white-capped waters and opposing swells
Owning and embracing mists and spray
Breezes and hard, steady winds
With the grit of manifest shorelines and uncountable Anishinaabe
women

OGITCHIDAAKWEWAG

I will translate our name for you.
It means we are women who do big things.

We have given birth to the future from writhing rocks, swirling currents, snowstorms, and clouds of mosquitoes.
We hold up the earth, holding our breath, waiting each in turn to rest and gulp for cold, fresh air
While another of our warrior women slips in from below to take our place, briefly, in the geologic scheme of things.

I will translate our name for you.
It means we have been here forever.

We do not need to speak of yesterday or of tomorrow in mere chalky words or algae-choked promises.
We live in the present and raise our children in the knowledge that other times and places are understood,
Like bedrock and compressed volcanic ash. We are the wave-polished agates that filled small voids in Earth's lava history.

I will translate our name for you.
It means we are an essential part of the ecology of this place.

We are not merely visiting and camping out while fantasizing about playing Indian on an ancient landscape
While turning eyes away from urban landforms and modern socioeconomic priorities,
When our children know that we heaved and shaped this landscape long before continents collided and scattered DNA like pollen.

I will translate our name for you.
It means that we are strong and enduring.

We are turtles made of ice and snow, shifting seasonally and predictably, sheltering our families.

We are watchful lynxes, meaty cranes, dancing caribou, well-trained waterfowl, and mischievous snakes.

We eat windstorms for breakfast and cause bodies of water to splash toward the sky like hot cups of biology soup.

I will translate our name for you.

It means that we are biological forces with the strength of mountains.

We domesticated the landscape you see about you, burning its forests into submission, then planting grasses, wild nuts, and berries

While singing love songs to the clans that worshipped our skills at cultivation and threw as offerings their bodies at our cooking fires,

Screeching hawks, unstoppable schools of swarming fishes, raucous ponds full of trilling toads and puffed up frogs stealing warm breezes from dusks and dawns.

I will translate our name for you.

It means that we sing and dance up the seasons with regularity.

We are thunderbirds pushing fresh winds against old swells across ancient lakes.

We are ancestors holding dry lightning in one hand, balmy cloud-bursts in another,

Tossing pollen and dry leaves into the wide-open eyes of predators that turn curious heads when they hear us scream.

I will translate our name for you.

It means that we live forever.

We are the bearers of tradition, clan songs, and story, the engravers of stone fonts and bones as kitchen utensils.

We are the voices of the departed as they travel the night skies, disseminating beams of colored light

Upon the heads and shoulders of our children and their children's children, tetherers of our own consistent strength and beauty.

I will translate our name for you.
It means we are women who do big things.

Manhukaa

Big Hazel Loon lived two lakes over in a small pond named
Manhukaa,
Where Loons gathered for feasts and celebrations
In a house made of lily pad roots and hazelnut twigs.
You could hear young owls screeching until dawn,
While crayfish were served up on big platters with grubs and salt.

When the chick was little, they called her Little Hazel,
And she never thought twice when her parents took her to sing clan
songs all night long
With a grownup loon named Big Crazy Hazel.
They interjected Fish Clan songs into the mix, while they passed the
pipe
And stroked the girl's hair until she fell asleep in front of the moon's
embers.

Grownup Hazel was kind and patient with her namesake,
And Little Hazel was appreciative of every smile and kind word that
came her way.
She rode around on Big Hazel's back, sprouted feathers, and sang
until dawn,
Singing loud cooing calls back and forth across the lake and beyond
the horizon,
Licking fish slime and maple sugar from her fingertips.

Big Hazel Loon lived two lakes over in a small pond named
Manhukaa,
Where Loons gathered for feasts and celebrations
In a house made of lily pad roots and hazelnut twigs,
And both Hazels sang Maanhuk Dodaim songs, shaking rattles made
of birch bark,

Strong leaders and songstresses,
Women who watched over their lakes with long, loud, raucous calls.

That's what the Ojibwe called those women back then: Loons.
And Leaders, because Loons scattered in spring,
Then gathered in fall when feather-sheds left them flightless and vulnerable.
They enticed Loon men into guarding the mouths of the bays, taking turns through the night,
While the women sang and cried together in sweat lodges made of black mud
And feathers they pulled from their own breasts.

When Big Hazel and her husband were away from Lake Manhukaa,
Living in cities where jobs and hope were more abundant,
Little Hazel's parents would bring her to fish on Manhukaa.
A convoluted body,
Mirror image of the clans that lived there,
Mirror image of the Hazels who scattered from and were drawn to one another.

Hazel remembers catching fat bluegill on Manhukaa.
Fish Clan, heady and fighting for survival against worm and hook
before giving themselves up, like medicine, to Loon Clan feasts and songs.
Hazel remembers reeling them in and loving them hard through her childhood,
Sleeping close-in between their gills, cushioned by soft, swaying weedbeds,
Rocking gently to the clan songs of bullfrogs and toads.

Big Hazel Loon lived two lakes over in a small pond named Manhukaa,
Where Loons gathered for feasts and celebrations
In a house made of lily pad roots and hazelnut twigs,
Where Fish parents loved Little Hazel when Big Hazel was far away.

They scattered and gathered together with the seasons, those two,
Never sure when to sing which clan songs,
So, they sang them all
On the convoluted, muddy shores of Manhukaa.

Manidoogiizis

(Call It January If You Like)

This is a moonrise given to us by mysteries so strong that we dare not trivialize. Do you hear me? No nightfalls to count. No distracting sunlight reflected by moon bodies. Just thick sky currents heavy with wet; and cold stealing hoarded sunshine from the lakes. Physics guides our biology. Dark days. Long nights.

Yesterday you were a tall, yellow coyote, looking past me toward the next perceived threat. You looked over your shoulder from inside my skin, risking your essence for one more quick meal before winds again shifted, and hopes disappeared from another day's horizon. Then you loped sideways past the row of pines we'd planted to protect ourselves from too-warm winds. Hungry days. Hungry nights.

Memorize my mixed scents, Coy-Wolf, lost in exurbs, sniffing around bait piles . . . old rags recycling your Wolf-DNA into a compressible niche below your song's surface. A few quick centuries tried to claim supremacy over the countless ice ages that pressed your carbons into limestone, shinbones buried under condensed miles of January snowfalls. Dark days. Long nights.

Soil tilts into your axis, and you long for your yellow-eyed family, keepers of your own curriculum, dug up from under Model Ts and sterile allotments; Hunting Songs subdivided under Internal Combustion Pop Tunes echo through your underbrush. Look, how you want to be long-legged, bred in desperation, wanting for better times stored away, submitting to fuel injected winters. Loud days. Desperate nights.

Coy-Wolf, your blood sidesteps identity's obligations in steel-toothed traps, springs swinging shut, tearing gray remnants from your anklebones. Clan Songs slide down your throat like fur, before you chew off the chorus you sang as a child. Saving yourself hides you downwind like a spore. Dark days. Long nights.

Hot and Cold rise on their haunches, mouths open and yelping for the continuity capacity of your Coy-Wolf fragile Clan Song. Moles burrow to the surface in dim-eyed confusion, responding to friction-induced heat. They would give up their body fat to save the Song, burrow upward to save seeds from overexposure to heavy suns. Dark burrows. Safe nights.

I saw a dark, vulnerable rabbit stubbornly refusing to shed its brown coat for a predominantly snowy one, willing to become winter breakfast in lieu of the Clan Song; and I saw you, Coy-Wolf, zigzagging through cold, loose crystals blowing hard over leafcrust. I heard snowbanks moan under the filtered sun and turn dislocated shoulders toward prevailing winds, composted leaves black on their breath. Dark days. Long nights.

Broad-shouldered moles absorb the sunshine then spit it out.

Painted Dancers

There was an overhang in the rocks by the highway.
I found it when my car broke down right next to it
On a curve in modernity where no aboriginal woman should stop.

It faced the east, where there had been a steep ravine
Carved by millennia of ice and trickling waterways
In an intermingled dance with desiccating winds where no fresh
waters should pause.

It must have been high above the streambed centuries ago,
Maybe even only fifty years earlier,
Before progress laid down there like an aboriginal woman in an
asphalt dress,

Like she was headed to a bar in Albuquerque or Sault Ste. Marie,
Where Indian women were twirled around to the beat of a jukebox,
Their dark hair let loose and swirling in and out of twentieth-century
nights.

It used to be a dirt road that crossed the creek
And only allowed access to the twentieth century when springmelts
faded away
And morning sun sent long tickling fingers into mountains' narrow
crevices.

When I got out of my car to pray for its safety, I saw paintings under
the rock ledge.
They were Indians all in a row dancing with other Indians,
And no jukebox, just layers of kaolin and ochres between rock
canvases.

And I knew that for a long time, Indian women and men had been shaded in that overhang
When they broke down and needed to climb away from the beating sounds
Of their own hearts and people who put demands upon them daily.

I picked a little bit of light green pigment from a thin horizontal layer
And tucked it into the pouch of my hooded sweatshirt
So that I could be an aboriginal woman again, dancing in green with no jukebox.

I wondered if someone would ever find me under that overhang,
Fingering smooth red and yellow ochres and praying for the twentieth century
To paint me more than asphalt hair and a bar pay phone among strange lumbermen.

The dancers looked so unencumbered, like they didn't need to make it into town.
They looked like they didn't need to get to a job or university
Or to try to make themselves something more than ochre dancers in the rocks.

I wondered if before modernity's dynamite, people passed under that overhang
Every day, from household to water source, from work to play,
From sunrise to sunset, just belonging there, free to stop, or even to dance.

I slid into narrowed rockways, away from the oppression of mounded paving
And I whittled away at ochre to paint my eye sockets and cheekbones,
But did not dare to paint myself dancing without twentieth-century expectations.

I drove for lifetimes trying to find that overhang again,
Where pigments wanted to dance on my skin
And waterways begged aboriginal women and men to stop and paint
our dancing presence.

Wanted to Be Born

Before she was born,
She kicked so much that people said
She really wanted to be born.

So, when she was born,
They named her that,
And as is the way with Ojibwe people,
They added a suffix that said,
"And here she is."

Ta da!
Look at this, she's right here . . .
And they even punctuated the statement
With a glottal stop right in the middle
To emphasize her presence and beauty
And to draw attention
To the beautiful mothers
Who gave birth to her.

There was no other way
To look upon her arrivals
As anything other than gifts.

So, they danced and sang
All around those ripe red wombs
That birthed her,
Turning first to the east
And then to the west
While her mothers rested
In anticipation of birthing her again.

Turtles pushed against gravity,
Uplifting soils and pebbles,
Sucking at her toes
In anticipation
Of her first lilting footstep
Into sacred waters.

Domesticated dogs
Reclined at her doorway
And panted out love songs
That they had practiced in unison
Since before their domestication.

Mink sent out long squealing chatters
Among their kindred,
An annunciation,
Then shed their skins,
Laid them at the feet of her mothers,
And quietly lay
In front of cooking fires
As endowments.

Big brown bats
Licked mosquitoes and pestilence
From her airspace,
Warriors
With long traditions of protecting
Those who chose to be born here,
To expectant civilizations
And sun-heated rocks full of windsongs.

Minnows
Leapt into the mouths of whitefish,
Who in turn
Threw themselves into the nets
Of her fathers and mothers

As they feasted in celebration
Of her desire to be among them.

In the nearby muskegs,
Wild cottons
Transformed their blooms
Into soft twining fibers
That floated on breezes,
Declaring themselves available
For the swaddling of generations.

Loons shed their feathers
And huddled together
In the bays that birthed her,
Posted lookouts each night,
And cooed long celebratory calls
Year after year
While she grew tall and strong,
With shoulders broad enough to support granite
And long seaweed fingers
For scattering spawn
Of salamanders and toads.

Cold Woman

That girl over there, the one with five-thousand-year-old sunlight
reflecting in her eyes,
They say she never learned to walk like most babies do.
She started dancing with her first step, skittering over ice crystals to
the musical howling of strong, unencumbered winds
And waves pounding against hollow volcanoes made of ice, all along
the sandy shorelines of downstream coves hidden among black rocks.

I heard that her first words were laughter made of blowing dry snow
that tinkles across cold, flat surfaces
And around bends in pinks and greens of granite architecture.
Her playground was constructed of curving polar gusts that protected
her dependence upon the regularity of arctic gifts.
She played with giant balls of cold moisture and fashioned writing
implements out of nothing but crystals stitched together into lace.

People tell long winter stories about the floral patterns of calico
fashioned from centuries of pounding, angled sleet
That her family hand stitched into parkas she pulled over oil-tanned
leggings
Colored with icy beads bored out on long, still nights,
While her grandmothers sang storm songs about frozen lakes and
times to travel across thick, safe highways made of solid forever.

She wore high-top slippers made of clear blue ice, with shiner
minnows and curled snails frozen in decorative motifs along the
outlines of her toes and anklebones.
Every February, she would slide through sunshine puddles over mile-
thick ice.
Afterward, her aunties made her warm teas out of heathers and small
seeds,

Then caribou and shaggy-skinned bears breathed warm moisture across her brow while she napped between seasonal storms.

She has mittens made from animal fat melted and dipped in cold water to congeal in protective layers
So that her fingers can rest between drumbeats that she taps out on membranes made of otters' bladders.
She knows songs that are rooted in the floors of ancient seas and weave back and forth from east to west,
First softly, then in crescendos, with long rests between wingbeats as the notes glide on strong thermal winds seeking nightfall.

I saw her one time, resting on a north-facing hillside, where my mother's brother harvested ice
To chill fish eggs until tomorrow's breakfast.
I stood back in safety and watched him cut away at her thigh with an agate knife blade worn loose from a grinding moraine,
While flakes of stone-hard water flew out against summer's solstice and vaporized into a dusty mist.
He sang constant thank-you songs to her, each with a long, loud chorus about her skills at compressing time and moisture into solid landforms.

Some nights, my whole family sings soft, gentle lullabies about that girl's rhythmic footfalls.
We pocket air molecules that are compressed into thickness under boreal skies.
Feathers, small branches, and soft barks we pound into fabrics to insulate sacred stories that we keep bundled up until warm clouds subside
And temperatures drop so low that rocks and lakes embrace one another in a slow, cool dance
Made of stars pressed close together with only small empty spaces for our heartbeats.

LISTEN TO YOUR GRANDMOTHER

All I wanted to do was to pick some mint, you know, the kind that grows wild and opportunistically,
The kind that makes your eyes tear when you steep it midmorning
After cleaning the ashes out of the bottom of the woodstove and coaxing life into snow-covered dry hardwood logs from the red coals deep in your belly.

I had paddled half a lifetime up and down the coast at the base of old mountains shaped like my grandmother and her sisters,
Where they'd dipped their long toes into cold springmelts and then left them there for my mom and me to find respite
In their narrow coves where clay and soft sands harbor wild irises by the thousands.

Sometimes the mint grew there for years, and other times it migrated to another inlet,
Behind a shallow island somewhere, begging us to get curious enough to find it.
We have a special relationship like that with that mint; it teases us,

And when we find that it has gifted us with its presence, we take a little bit of it from here and there,
Careful to leave enough white toothy roots to cast themselves out upon another adventure
Out behind the cape, where even crows tell us not to venture, unless the winds are asleep in a canyon between inland basins, gambling together like old men,
Betting on tadpoles and shallow-rooted greens.

I paddled up there one day, and I got lost in a crevice,
Following day campers who had wandered north from their nearest urban security.

So I backpaddled into a dark space, under overhanging roots from a tenacious black spruce.

The old tree had been singing a song that I recognized from my childhood, sinuous like its rock-wrapping roots.
It was a song based in complex mathematical rhythms that started with soft waves against lakeside rocks,
The tempo tied in steadfast knots to the prevailing wind, rising and falling like the emotional movements of an opera that lasted for days or months.

Then the rhythms divided and subdivided like the finest roots of that spruce tree until I got lost in the infinite combinations of sounds
And had to rest my head on wet, sweet-smelling mosses
Which were as opportunistic and persistent as the mint shoots I'd sought out at the beginning of my journey.
I don't remember how long the opera lasted, because I dozed off in the comfort of the soft spaces between crescendos.

I heard the shuffling of feet and the rustling of recycled plastic windbreakers as the crowds flowed back toward their tents and their automobiles
Through well-lit aisles carved out by chainsaws and earthmovers,
Oblivious to the clan songs and textbooks buried under their deeds to the continents.

I remember that the old ladies started shifting then, having waited for the crowds to move inland toward the highways;
They rolled over all at once and faced into the narrow cove where I'd been waiting for respite,
And they poured stories out of themselves all at once, thick and heavy with the scent of fresh balsam growth.

If I hadn't been paying attention for several thousand years, I might have mistaken their words for mist,
Flowing down their hillsides and snaking valleys,

Like heavy, cool air unable to hold on to its burden of moisture.

I might have mistaken the outpouring for a predictable summer's shift of molecular density
Instead of hearing the predictable movement of their long histories and stories about my birth
That they had shared with my family for as long as we could remember.

My grandmother showed me an inscribed band that had been affixed with metal screws to the igneous underside of her wrist;
It was the tattooed number they had used to keep track of her at the boarding school where they planned to teach her to stop behaving like a mountain,
To start speaking like a flat, Midwestern wheat field: domesticated, profitable, and calm.

Apparently, the matrons of the school could not differentiate between her and her mountain sisters
Or the sandy, shifting hillsides of scattered dunes or the duck-filled potholes of undulating prairies;
So, they instructed the girls to put away their windsong harmonies and to sing slowly, in unison, forsaking crescendos,

Such as the revelations of crows calling hawks to open up a sweet carcass so that they all could feast
Or the pounding of hard, high waves out of the west as they pulled spores and insects out of treetops
And sent them to distant bays that sang love songs in desperation for seasonal lovers to fulfill their biological destiny.

So those girls crept out at night, and they swam across landscapes of air thick with dust and desperation,
Breast-stroked from island to island until they reached hidden pockets of mainland safe with dense brush,
And they climbed all the way home, slow and steady, a grain at a time.

Sometimes they dissolved themselves into red irons and green coppers, desperately leaching themselves into puddles,
Where they waited patiently for sunrises with long arms of heat to evaporate their hopes into thin streams of perfection, clustering together as clouds,
Carrying them home to build themselves back into mountains of prosperity and windborne ideas bigger than survival.

They told me these things over the course of several generations—so many that I can't count.
They instructed me how to bundle up those stories into bedrock, how to alternate them with coarse gravel and empty spaces
So that there would be room for the crescendos created by small, sticky plants that eat insects smaller than grains of sand.

They told me to make diagrams in books made of generations, lessons written down with flours pounded from roots,
Songs echoed by deep valleys and mounded hillsides in traditional harmonies carved out by watersheds,
Birthing new singers of songs cradled in the arms of my sisters,
Long boughs and hungry roots, twisting around rocks and empty spaces, teaching lessons made from obstacles.

One time, between windy spells on the shoreline, I dipped my fingers into the city to feel for currents and perceptions,
To leach out long, unpredictable choruses from even longer growth spurts of oral histories and cautionary tales.
I was hungry to share the responsibility of speaking for my grandmothers in words that fumble into mere mumblings and insecurities . . .

A woman wearing a long gown woven from ships' ballast beckoned me over with a wave of her opera glasses,
And she told me that the first two chapters were too hard to read because they made her cry;

Only, I thought that singing our stories was supposed to be about making me cry
In between laughing and gulping up calm breezes in the empty spaces when rocks themselves pause for breath.

I wanted to tell her that I always want to cry when I listen to crows lamenting the loss of carrion to an eagle
Or when pebbles make me stop and listen to a long, slow tale between lifetimes of breathing in strong, hot teas;
But my mouth was full of silt, and no thoughts came out fast enough to satisfy her impatience

With Indian authors and old Indian stories,
Stories that take lifetimes to tell in between the incessant sighs of cliffs shedding lichens,
Stories that defy the permanence of words on paper or electrical impulses bent between sheets of glass.
We sing these songs when we pause between strides and heartbeats to listen to old mountains weep and sigh.

How Alice B. Marten Spends Her Days

Alice B. Marten waits . . .

For starfalls on clear, cold nights, for thousand-foot-deep lake basins to cool down from their summers of partying, then dancing far too late into autumn, with choppy two-bit waves grilling beefsteaks on her windowsill. They toss up their body heat to the North Wind, then roll themselves flat and succumb; head down south for some okra and tomatoes from the lips of succulent swamp girls.

Alice B. Marten tosses . . .

Through her nighttimes, looking for breaks in the cloud cover, where Marten boys bat around constellations with cedar paddles, chasing each other in and out of cloudbanks and the shadows of aggressive spruce trees that gouge at them and throw midnights in uncontrolled handfuls, until the youngsters lose interest and trail home with dawns in their pockets.

Father Marten displays . . .

Four deadfall traps he pulls from hungry tree-lines each dusk, clearing experienced pathways for Martens to play, smiles at his own history of competence, fur bundles piled up on his living room couch, exhausted ribcages rising and sinking predictably, smiling boys with perch minnows on their breath, carelessness folded into their palms and knock-knock jokes tucked into beaded pouches around their slim necks.

Alice B. Marten empties . . .

Ashes from the woodstove by candlelight, cleans the litter box, pries bits of Marten fur from the sink drain, puts away dry dishes, replaces the broken top on the red enameled percolator, hauls in firewood, thaws field mice for supper, bakes thick biscuits, then pulls a wide-mouth pint of blackberry jam from a shelf underneath the bench where jumbled fur-lined mittens and boots steam themselves dry. She inhales the perfume of wet fur with each sip of hot coffee thick with canned milk.

Alice B. Marten sifts . . .

For silence between obligations, weaves bedclothes out of used-up down jackets, and bleeds heat on the narrow path between her house and the world. She wipes sawdust and empty cocoons from her ceiling beams, nibbles on toasted squash seeds, and paws through glaciers for dry sands to scatter on her icy doorstep before throwing electricity into the wind and setting mousetraps for spare change along the dusty floorboards.

Alice B. Marten worries . . .

Because she tries to open up heavy skies to soft cries from chickadees on brittle bare branches that once swelled with growth buds. Some days, they scold upward with her in predictable little clicks, before they settle in to cry softly in low, drawn-out murmurs, depositing thick mucus between her lips. Alice B. swallows salt and cries out loud during each chorus; then she listens through her stovepipe for smoky sounds of encouragement.

Alice B. Marten shouts . . .

Out loud, because she has misplaced her travel map to cool, soft breezes on isolated hillsides, where she has periodically run off to fertilize fast-growing balsams, burrowing to deposit her fear in dark sands under the punk wood of rotting stumps. Her college diploma came with a disclaimer that it lost its value when pinned to the tail of a dancing Marten, and she wants to scotch-tape that sentiment to a whirlwind and stuff it back into the warren from which it seeped.

Alice B. Marten pulls . . .

Flesh from the small bones of her breast and spine that she has simmered overnight while badgers hissed at her windowpanes. She twists the small muscles into fibers that she blends with steamed lambsquarters, then weaves a soft backpack that she climbs into between household chores. Once inside her own weaving, she insulates her toes with baking soda and smooth white macaroni from an urban food bank, ties herself shut, then throws away her consciousness.

Alice B. Marten scratches . . .

Small, simple recipes with short claw marks onto moist sheets of inner cambium birch bark that she trims with sweetgrass, stitched in place with strong sinews from her own long jumping muscles, and she folds each bark segment onto itself like a Jacob's ladder, then packs them under bushels of red flint corn that her grandfather grew during his childhood and stored away for future lifetimes.

Alice B. Marten filters . . .

Ashes from the floors around her cookstove into her old coffee-pot, where she softens corn kernels and hazelnuts into grits that she serves for breakfast on cold, clear mornings when moonlight opens up opportunities like eggshells and begs Martens to pray in empty spaces between tall pines and dancing skies. She lubricates her tired joints with tallow from her own belly and slips out between constellations for a quick twirl with Father Marten, then rushes home to nap under fogbanks before fools discover she has gazed up past their furrowed foreheads.

Alice B. Marten harvests . . .

Wild grass seeds from plants she grows on a shelf above her cook-stove, and she sautés them over high heat in oils she has rendered from beechnuts, coaxing them down from their tree nests with sharp cold snaps and breezes, stealing them away from deer trails, or bartering caches from red squirrels with her store of ripe apples that she chills in her barns made of deadfalls. She pours fresh birch sap over the brown-ing seeds, then simmers them with a half-pint of summer solstice and dried herbs from an overgrazed field. When the kernels are soft and plump, Alice B. curls herself up around the skillet to keep it warm until nightfall, and she sings herself a soft, sad song about sweeping floors.

Alice B. Marten mixes . . .

Thousand-year-old leftover dried beans with snippets of wild onions and melts store-bought cheese in an old iron skillet. She serves this with fried bits of red cornmeal ground smooth on a piece of pre-heated lava she stores under her pillow at night to take the chill off the blankets after Martens bat around constellations with cedar paddles, barking out adolescent epithets and sculpting one another's muscles and skills, until they pant in unison and fall from the sky into soft Marten burrows and moist kitchen smells.

Alice B. Marten soaks . . .

Dark purple corn leaves in warm amniotic fluids, then twists their strong fibers into coiled cylindrical baskets in which she stores old dreams and condensed fish breath pressed hard into solid cakes of ingenuity that she stacks on shelves between her mason jars and old textbooks. Sometimes, she takes out the baskets before sunrise and rubs their oily essence onto the calluses between her toes and her ambition, smoothing fat into the cracks in her skin, where she has pulled out her own fur to weave rope ladders up to the stars.

Alice B. Marten taps out . . .

Confident songbeats between freezes and thaws, pattering a cast-iron burner with a dried balsam twig, rasping ash logs against one another for long, slow back harmonies and skittering sheets of broken ice across puddles for crescendos. She sings loud choruses to the ghosts of dogs, shakes dried lentils inside an empty birch shell, then throws pebbles against her outside windows. Old South Wind creeps down her driveway for a peek, throws pine cones at the roof, and hums along between gasps.

Alice B. Marten empties . . .

Ashes from the woodstove by candlelight, cleans the litter box, scoops up bits of Marten fur from the bases of chair legs, scours breakfast dishes, packs lunches, mops the walls, cures sweetgrass for weaving baskets, washes and sorts mismatched Marten-fur socks, fries up lake trout with cornmeal, paints portraits of Martens on birch bark with porcupine quills, skitters to and from the post office, makes tall jars of cherry lemonade, and pays her taxes. After a quick cup of coffee, she dances around her kitchen table twice. Then she sits down to weave predictability into open vessels, and waits for starfalls.

ACKNOWLEDGMENTS

Poems from this collection have been published previously as follows:

"Cranberry-Picking Season," *The Goose*, Spring 2019.
"The Last Caribou," *The Goose*, Fall 2019.
"Biboon Was a Friend of Mine," *Waters Deep: A Great Lakes Poetry Anthology, Split Rock Review*, Fall 2018.
"Desperation Cookies,"
"Listen to Your Grandmother,"
"Wild Raspberries in the Rain," *Yellow Medicine Review*, Fall 2017.

ABOUT THE AUTHOR

Lois Beardslee is an Anishinaabe (Lake Superior Ojibwe, a.k.a. Chippewa Indian) author and illustrator from northwest Lower Michigan. She grew up between northern Michigan and remote family bush camps in northern Ontario, hunting caribou and moose in the arctic watershed and fishing seasonally from a small island on the north shore of Lake Superior, while also attending college and graduate school. Her work addresses institutionalized racism and stereotypes in literature. While celebrating the strength and endurance of Native Americans, she specifically looks at how racism in the field of education affects Native American communities. She has won several awards for both writing and civil rights, including ForeWord and IPPY bronze medals, and is the author of several books, including *The Women's Warrior Society*.